INVISIBLE JEWS

SURVIVING THE HOLOCAUST IN POLAND

By

Eddie Bielawski

Edited for publication by

Jack Cohen

Third edition

ISBN: 978-1976075933

Cover design by Jack Cohen

"Chance favors the prepared mind."

Louis Pasteur

Contents

Figures

Dedication

I dedicate these memoirs to my parents, **Yitzhak Yehiel** and **Paula (Pessia) Bielawski**, without whose brains, foresight, bravery and dedication we would never have survived.

Preface

No one who wasn't there can understand what it was like. No one who hasn't experienced gnawing hunger – not just for hours or days, but for months – can understand what it was like to survive under those conditions. Nor to survive a Polish winter in a barn or in an underground bunker with no heat, and only straw and a few rags to keep you from freezing to death. No one who hasn't sat for days in the same position, not able to move for fear of making a noise, the tiniest of noises. No one who hasn't experienced it can know what it was like as a child not to be able to play or even to cry. Throughout the whole three years, from 1941 when the Nazis started the deportations and the mass killings and we began to hide, until 1944, when we were liberated by the Russians, no one can understand what it was like to become invisible, to become invisible Jews.

We were in a totally hostile environment. No one could be trusted. There were Poles who would kill us, steal all that we had, or turn us over to the Germans for a reward and to see us dead. The Germans themselves or their Ukrainian helpers would torture and humiliate us and would murder us without any hesitation or flicker of humanity. Everyone was starving as food was scarce; but for us, food was rare, we lived on a starvation diet. Don't ask me how we survived. It seems impossible, but we did. We could only survive by bribery and sheer persistence and luck.

There was the occasional Pole who showed human feelings towards us, who fed us and risked his life and that of his family to help us for a time. But they were few and far between. The only way we could, in fact, survive without being shot, murdered, or captured and deported to Treblinka was to become invisible. It is a tribute to my father and his brothers that we did manage to do this. We were treated like vermin. And for what? What had we done to them that was so bad that they should treat us this way?

Why did it take me all these years to write these memoirs? There are many reasons. Canadian Jews in 1948 (when we first came to Canada) were reluctant to hear Holocaust stories, so we stopped telling them. Secondly, I didn't want our past to destroy my future, so I sublimated my feelings – sort of, "let sleeping dogs lie." But the "dogs" were not sleeping, they were only dozing. So, as time went by, I began to think that at least my wife, children, and grandchildren should know our story.

At first, I thought that there were so many Holocaust stories out there, one more would not make much difference. But I slowly began to change my mind. Every story is unique and must be preserved for future generations. Especially since the generation which experienced our near annihilation is almost gone, and the number of Holocaust deniers is on the rise.

I have a number of people to thank for helping me gather the courage and willpower to put pen to paper.

First of all, my wonderful wife, Elaine, for convincing me to write my story. She knew when to push and when to back off. She did all the typing for me and had many suggestions on how to improve the expression of some of my ideas.

Secondly, I would like to thank my sister, Rene, for filling me in on some of the events of the early years of the war which I was too young to remember or which she clarified, and also for putting together the timeline I used on p. 72.

Thirdly, I would like to acknowledge the help I received from my Uncle Shraga Feivel Bielawski's book, *"The Last Jew from Wegrow"* (Praeger, 1991).

Last but not least, I would like to thank my good friend Jack Cohen for nudging me into turning my memoirs into a book. He not only edited and organized my work into chapters, but also thought up the title and gave me invaluable advice. He stood by me from beginning to end.

Eddie Bielawski, Netanya, 2017

Strategies for Survival

What strategies could a Jew take to look after his family and try to survive under the conditions that existed in Poland and elsewhere in Europe during WWII? Given that the Jews had no military training and could not obtain weapons (the Polish National Army was so anti-Semitic that they would not sell guns to Jews and would more likely kill them). The only two options were to run and to hide.

Some Jews realized that the Germans were rounding up Jews in villages where they lived and also in towns and cities using lists of names (usually organized and printed on IBM machines). So, to avoid being rounded up and transported, it was necessary to get away and leave the Jewish areas before the round-up took place. It was also necessary not to have an address that could be found on a resident's list. It might seem obvious in retrospect, but if a Jew wanted to avoid being rounded up, he and his family had to leave their home and find a place to live or hide where they would not be sought or found by the Germans and their many collaborators. Of course, this was a difficult and perilous thing to do in a totally hostile environment and depended on luck and chance.

In order to survive, it was necessary to plan ahead. Mr. Yitzhak Bielawski sold everything he had and converted all his money into gold dollars. With this, he could bribe the Polish peasants to obtain food and a place to hide, whatever happened to the value of the zloty. Of course, the gold coins had to be hidden because of bandits and hostile Polish peasants, so they sewed them into bands around the limbs of their baby son, Eddie, the author, who was never searched.

It was also necessary to find a really effective hiding place or "bunker." They used two kinds, either basically a hole in the ground in the middle of a field that was big enough for ten people, or a carefully constructed small room, where ten people could hide all day and not be detected in a fairly normal search. They also had to be able to come out at night to walk around and to eat and relieve themselves. This also required that the Poles were paid enough or owed enough not to turn them in for the reward.

Such were the conditions under which people survived, remaining essentially invisible. But, the conditions were intolerable, filthy, unhealthy and dangerous. It is a miracle that a family of ten could survive under these conditions. Yet, they did. It is an indelible stain on so-called European civilization based on Christianity that this was the conditions under which millions of Jews were murdered and few survived. Terrible crimes against humanity were perpetrated on a daily basis throughout Europe. Yet now, these same people give us advice on how to protect human rights. What hypocrisy!

What distinguishes this extraordinary narrative of survival through the Holocaust from some others is the fact that this resourceful man, Yitzhak Bielawski, managed, through bribery and persuasion, to keep his whole family safe and alive. And most incredibly, he built bunker after bunker and hiding place after hiding place where, for three long years (1941-44), they managed to endure the suffering and deprivation. With incredible endurance, they came out of it in the end with great resilience to eventually restart their lives in a new and more tolerant and hospitable environment.

Jack Cohen, Netanya, 2017

Prologue

In October 1943, after months of running and hiding, the Bielawski brothers spoke to Bujalski and convinced him that if they could build a hiding place in the barn in such a way that he couldn't find it, he would let us stay – for a very large payment in gold, of course. Well, he agreed.

The loft in the barn was very long, so the brothers built a false wall inside the loft, just a few feet from the outside wall. Bujalski supplied the building materials. They built the wall in the same manner as the original wall and made sure it looked dirty and old so that it would not arouse suspicion.

The entrance was a moveable floor plank which could only be reached by a ladder from the barn. When we were all up there, we would pull the ladder up, replace the plank and be invisible. It seems that the only way that a Jew could survive in wartime Poland was to be invisible.

When the job was finished and most of us were in our hiding place, Bujalski was called. He searched and searched, but could not find us. He then called his wife, Helena. She too searched but could find nothing. They really didn't believe that we were there. When they were shown where we were, they were satisfied with the arrangements and agreed to keep us.

I. Becoming Invisible
Background

I was born in the town of Wegrow (pronounced *Wengrov*) in north-eastern Poland in mid-1938. Not a propitious time and place for a Jewish child to be born.

Wegrow is located in eastern Poland, about 70 kilometers from Warsaw and 20 kilometers from Treblinka. It is an ancient town, first mentioned in the 14th century. The Jews were invited during the 16th century, and they made their living in tax farming and commerce.

Before the war, the Jews (although mostly very poor) led a rich cultural and political life. Their political allegiance varied from Communists, Bundists, various shades of Zionists, to the Ultra-Orthodox.

The population at the outset of the war was 16,000 people, of whom about 6,000 were Jews. At the height before the liquidation (on September 22, 1942), the number of Jews had risen to 8,300, as many had been brought into the Wegrow Ghetto from the surrounding areas.

When the German army was approaching Wegrow in early September 1939, my family left town and stayed in a small village called Pienki, a few kilometers away, and stayed with a village elder for a few days. When we heard that the town had fallen without much of a fight, we returned to our home. (Where else could we go?)

Soon after, the Nazis marched into Wegrow. In October 1939, they forcibly took a great deal of Jewish property. Among the goods that were confiscated was the lumber in my father's lumber yard.

My mother went to see a German officer about it. She explained that she had two small children at home and no means of sustenance since our lumber had been seized. My mother told us that he was an older man who was sympathetic and he told her that he too had children in Germany, and he released the lumber. I wonder if that officer could have been Captain Wilm Hosenfeld (born in 1895). He was the officer who later saved the life of Wladislav Szpilman, the Polish Jewish pianist in the Warsaw Ghetto (made famous in the film *"The Pianist"*). Hosenfeld was honoured posthumously by Yad Vashem in Jerusalem on February 16, 2009 as a Righteous among the Nations. His profile fits – he was in his forties, sympathetic and helpful and he was stationed in Wegrow from late 1939 to December 1940 – but I will never know for sure if he was the same man.

The Germans did not immediately start to murder Jews. They first had to get organized, then they dehumanized the Jewish population little by little, until the "final solution." They imposed a curfew on the Jews, confiscated Jewish property, and made Jews wear white armbands with a blue

Star of David identifying them as Jews. They took them for hard labour whenever they felt like it and could beat and kill Jews with impunity, and they finally sent whoever was left to concentration camps and death camps.

My sister, Rene, who was born on Sept. 6, 1932, was seven years old when the war broke out (I was only 16 months old). She managed to complete Grade I, but never made it to Grade II. It would take another six years until she could return to school.

My parents used to sneak into a Jewish neighbour's apartment at night (thus breaking the curfew) to listen to the news from around the world. Radios were forbidden, and had my parents and neighbours been caught listening to an illegal radio and breaking the curfew, the consequences would have been terrible.

They hoped to hear that the Allies were winning the war and that we would soon be rescued, but their hope was in vain. The war was not going very well and my parents realized that it would still last a long time.

I, of course, had no knowledge of what my parents were doing, but my sister told me how she stayed awake, scared sick until she heard the door open.

Before the war, we lived with our maternal grandmother, Gittel, and her husband, Mendele Laufer. Their house was in a non-Jewish area of town and consisted of three apartments, two of which belonged to our grandparents. At first, we occupied the larger of the two apartments but the

Germans forced us to move into the smaller one and moved a family of refugees into the larger one.

There were many horrors that the Germans inflicted on the Jews, but one especially stands out in my mind, one that my mother and father witnessed and recounted to me many times.

On Yom Kippur, 1939, the Germans forced the town rabbi, Rabbi Jacob Mendel Morgenstern (*Figure 1*) of blessed memory, who was dressed in his holiday robes, and "Streimel" (a special fur hat worn by Orthodox Jews), out into the street. They assembled all the Jews and made them watch as they forced their religious leader to dance and then to sweep the street and gather the horse manure in his Streimel, and then they stabbed him. He later died, as he was a diabetic. All this happened on the holiest day of the year.

All I have stated up to this point is a background of which I have no memory, but was witnessed by my parents and sister.

Figure 1: Rabbi Yaakov Mendel Morgenshtern.

First Experiences

Having been born in mid-1938 in Poland, I am probably one of the youngest Holocaust survivors with any memory of the war years. This is not a history – I'll leave that to the historians. It is simply a recounting of the events as seen through the eyes of a young child.

Figure 2. The four Bielawski brothers in 1940. Left to right: Yitzhak, Feivel, Yerahmiel and Moshe, wearing white armbands with the Star of David.

My immediate family consisted of my father, Yitzhak, my mother, Paula, my sister, Rene – six years my senior – and me. My mother was an only child whose father had died when she was only two years old, and my grandmother, who was a very beautiful young woman, was left destitute with a small child. Her economic plight forced her into a loveless marriage with a much older man. They never had any children. My father was the oldest of five children: four brothers (*Figure 2*) and a sister. His father, a sickly man, many years my grandmother's senior, had died before I was born. His mother – my paternal grandmother – ran the household. My father's family had a small menswear store in the centre of town, so they were considered well off. In truth, it only meant that they weren't destitute, which I suppose was no small achievement in those times and under those circumstances..

My father's mother was a very pious woman who was against my father marrying my mother, in spite of the fact that she was beautiful and relatively well-educated, both in religious as well as secular subjects. She simply was not wealthy, religious enough, nor did she have "*yichus*" – i.e., she was not the scion of a rabbi or known Torah scholar.

Figure 3: My mother Paula in 1946

Nevertheless, my father, the oldest brother, was a very independent, stubborn man who would not be swayed; and my parents married in 1930. My sister was born in September 1932, and I was born in May 1938.

I would like to mention that before the War, my father, who was an ambitious man, was engaged in various small enterprises. He had a lumberyard in Wegrow, a dry goods outlet in Warsaw, and in the summer, he ran a resort in Urle, a few kilometers outside of Warsaw.

I was a very blond, almost white-haired child, and my mother was a light-skinned, green-eyed woman (*Figure 3*), so when I was with her, we could pass as Aryans. Only later did I realize the significance of that.

Figure 3: Eddie (the author) at age 8 in 1946.

My father (*Figure 4*), on the other hand, was almost a caricature of a Jew – short, thin, with a large "Jewish" nose.

Figure 4: Yitzhak Bielawski in 1926

No way could he pass for anything but what he was.

My maternal grandmother, Gittel (*Figure 5*), spent a lot of time at our house. I remember that I adored her, and she just loved being with her two only grandchildren. I especially enjoyed her taking me to the town bakery to pick up the "cholent" (a stew made of meat, potatoes, barley, etc., which is usually cooked overnight on a slow fire). That is why it was taken to the bakery, because there was always a hot oven there. The baker was usually given a small sum of money for his services. I remember the bakery well. Its ovens were below ground level, and the bakers used long paddles to put in and take out the hot bread and the earthenware pots of cholent.

Figure 5. Gitel, my maternal grandmother (left: the only known photograph of her, rescued from my mother's locket).
Sarah Freida, my paternal grandmother (right: in 1940). She died in 1946 and was buried in Poland, but in 1974 she was reinterred in Israel.

About two years after the Nazis had taken firm control of Wegrow, my parents and we two children were forced to move into a small house in a Christian neighbourhood on the outskirts of town.

I, of course, couldn't understand what was happening. I only knew that we weren't living at home anymore. I remember seeing many smartly uniformed men in the streets that my parents viewed with fear – but to me, they were only very exotic looking strangers.

My grandmother Gittel was even worse off than we were, as she and her husband had been relocated by the Germans and were given a small cubicle in a large room that had been partitioned off by heavy curtains. They had almost no privacy and I was frightened to go there; it was dingy and smelled bad.

I had no understanding as to what was going on, but I felt the terrible tension and fear all around. I couldn't understand why the Jews spoke to each other in whispers nor why they never visited each other's homes anymore. What I do remember vividly is my father disappearing for long periods of time. Only later did I learn that he had been travelling to the Warsaw Ghetto. (Many years later, he explained to me that, at first, the Warsaw Ghetto was guarded but not hermetically sealed, and one could get in and out if one was quick and resourceful.)

I don't even want to speculate what the penalty for being caught was. In any case, he smuggled foodstuffs into the Ghetto and smuggled goods, such as cloth and leather, out of the Ghetto, which he would again trade for food and other necessities. It was on one of those trips when my father brought some food to the well-known Rabbi Yitzhak Menachem Danziger (*Figure 6*), the Alexander Rabbi (rabbis were known by the great yeshivot they founded; in this case, it was in the town of Alexandrovsk). The rabbi blessed him and said that although many Jews would perish in this war, he and his family would survive – and so it was. My father, although he came from a religious family (his

father was an Alexander Hassid), was not religious himself. It does, however, make one wonder.

Figure 6: Rabbi Yitzhak Menachem Danziger, the Alexander Rabbi

Another time, my father disappeared for an extended length of time. I believe it was over a month, and my mother feared that the worst had occurred. I later learned that he and his brother Feivel were trying to smuggle some clothes into the Russian-controlled territory and check out the possibility of all of us moving there to escape the Nazis. (Our town was situated about thirty-five miles from the Bug River which was the border between Russian and German territory according to the Ribbentrop-Molotov agreement.)

When they finally returned, my father told us what had happened. He and his brother were arrested by the Russians while crossing the Bug River and sent to a lockup, where they languished in squalor and starvation rations for about three weeks. When my father asked the guard with what crime they were being charged, the guard said that he didn't know. When asked who did know, the guard said that the officer who had arrested them knew, but that he had been transferred so there was no one who had the authority either to charge them or release them. It was truly a Kafkaesque situation.

Eventually, my father asked the guard if there was a Jewish officer in the vicinity. When the guard replied that there was, my father asked to see him. He gave the guard a small bribe (he apparently still managed to keep a bit of money on his person), and the guard brought the officer as agreed. My father then explained that he had done what he had done because he had a family back in Poland who were virtually starving. The officer pulled some strings and got them out. They learned that the economic situation on the other side of the river was no better than on our side, so he made his way back; and here he was, with no money and no goods.

Our situation steadily worsened and no one knew what to do. There were very few choices, and none good. I remember my mother and father whispering at night that they should have some sort of hiding place in case of an emergency.

Imagine the situation: you are a Jew living in a one-room apartment in an area inhabited almost exclusively by Polish Catholics who are not especially favourably disposed to you. In fact, many, if not most, are out and out anti-Semites who would like nothing better than to be rid of the Jews. How does one build a bunker under such circumstances? My father thought and thought but could find no solution. My uncles had prepared a hiding place in the attic of their house. They built a second brick wall beside the original one and indistinguishable from it, so that they could hide between the two walls. An entrance to the hiding place was built so that it was invisible from the outside. The only access to the attic itself was through a trap door with a retractable rope ladder. My father thought that perhaps we could go there in an emergency, but he realized that this was not a practical solution, as his family's hiding place was too far away, and in any case, it was too small to hold all of us.

The First Bunker

One night, my father had a dream (he told me about it many times over), and in this dream, he saw what he had to do: where to build the bunker, how to build it, and even its dimensions.

He would build a bunker under the middle one of three wooden storage sheds behind the house. It was the only shed that belonged to us. In his dream, he saw the bunker as a six-by-four-foot hole. Covered with boards, on top of which would be placed soil and bits of straw which would render it invisible. The entrance would be from inside "our" shed; it would be a one-and-a-half-foot square. In order to camouflage the entrance, he would construct a shallow box and fill it with earth and cover it with straw so that it would be indistinguishable from the rest of the earthen floor. Air would be supplied through a drain pipe buried in the earth, with one end in the bunker and the other end in a thicket of thistles in the nearby field. This was to be our Noah's Ark that would save us from the initial deluge. Now, all he had to do was build it – easier said than done.

Finally, he came up with a plan whereby he went out the back window at night, took the rusty lock off the shed door, and had my mother lock him in, so that anyone walking by would not see anything amiss.

My father had always been handy with tools, so he knew how to go about building the bunker. The big problem, besides the hard work, was the secrecy and the need for absolute silence while working.

Another problem was that it was absolutely essential that he have some time where he could make noise, because he had to nail the boards together that were to be our roof. He also had to saw and build the trap door. Of course, any noise would attract attention and ruin everything. Luckily for us, a fire happened to break out in town and all the neighbours ran toward the fire, shouting excitedly. There was a great uproar and a lot of noise. It was then that my Dad seized the opportunity to saw and hammer. He worked quickly and efficiently and managed to finish just before the commotion died down. It took my father about three weeks to finish the job. When he was done, he took my mother and sister into the shed and asked them if they could find the trap door. When they could not, he was satisfied.

Next, the inside of the bunker had to be prepared so that we could go there at a moment's notice. My mother prepared dry biscuits, jars of jam made out of beets, some tinned goods such as sardines, some sugar and salt. All the foodstuffs were placed in tins so that no worms or animals could get at them. We placed two buckets in the bunker.

One bucket was filled with water, the other bucket was empty and would serve as the latrine. We also took down some blankets, a couple of pillows and some warm clothing. We were ready.

As I said earlier, I knew nothing of the bunker. I only remember that our rations were becoming smaller and the general feeling of despair worsened. One thing that has been etched indelibly in my mind is the sight of the Nazi army marching toward Russia. Our house was located on the main road running toward the Russian frontier. Day and night, they marched – soldiers, trucks, tanks, and more soldiers in a never-ending line, marching as only Germans know how to march – an invincible force. I will never forget their marching songs and especially one which went:

Hi li hi lo hi la

Hi li hi lo hi la

Hi li hi lo

Hi la la la la la la la la

over and over again. I remember my father, holding me in his arms, saying to my mother, "Who is going to stop them? Certainly not the Russians."

The Russians had a reputation of being brave, but it was basically a rag-tag army of peasants. It was certainly no match for the well-oiled Nazi war machine. Our situation was hopeless. Up until September 1942, life was intolerable, but at least there was life. My father, who was an enormously resourceful man, managed to somehow feed us. A number of times, he was rounded up for work detail, but each time he managed to escape: either through bribes, or by ducking into an alley as they were being marched through town. As only two or three soldiers guarded all the men, they couldn't afford to go chasing after one man. That was his calculation, and it worked – although it didn't have to.

As I said earlier, life was intolerable. Jews could be beaten or killed on any pretext or no pretext at all. We were subject to the whims of the Germans and their many willing helpers with no recourse to any authority. The Jewish population of the town had swelled almost three-fold from its pre-war number, as more Jews from the surrounding areas were forced into Wegrow. As there was no living space, each room was crammed with one or two families. I had heard the word "Treblinka," although I had no idea what it meant except that it was a bad place. Only years later did I learn just how bad.

Monday, September 21, 1942 (the 10th of Tishrei according to the Hebrew calendar), Yom Kippur, was the last day that the Jews of Wegrow would know as a community. The day after Yom Kippur, I remember being yanked out of bed (it was about four in the morning) and rushed down, together with my father, mother and sister, into the bunker that my father had prepared. When the commotion began, my grandmother Gittel came and locked us in from the outside as we had previously arranged, and then she returned to her own place. I remember hearing shooting, shouting, screaming and cries of "*Shema Israel*" as we all sat still holding our breaths.

Later that morning, we heard Ukrainian voices. We were more afraid of the Ukrainians than of the Germans, if that was possible. It was their job to round up the Jews, put them in horse-drawn wagons and send them to Treblinka. They were referred to by us as the "black devils" because of the black uniforms they wore, and one could expect no mercy from them.

The black devils broke the rusty lock and came into the small shed. They looked around and started to bang their rifles on the ground, listening for a hollow sound.

As luck would have it, they stood on the trap door and hit the solid ground all around – but they didn't actually hit the trap door itself. I remember us just sitting there, helplessly holding our breaths. We were centimeters from death, but they left without finding our hiding place. Was this another of many miracles? Probably, but no doubt my father had done a wonderful job camouflaging the entrance to our bunker and filling the shed with all kinds of junk so that it would be difficult to enter and search.

The next day, all was quiet. We all understood what had happened, although not to what extent. We stayed put day after day in the small, stifling, damp bunker, the size of a grave. At night, my father would go out to empty the slop bucket and bring water.

When my grandmother Gittel returned to her room, the Ukrainians came and ordered her and her husband out. Her husband, Mendel Laufer, refused to leave and was shot on the spot. My grandmother managed to run away and hide in a nearby wheat field for a few days. She then came to check on our situation and stayed with us for a couple of nights.

Our bunker, however, was too small to accommodate all of us. It was crowded with the four of us – five was impossible – so my father sat in the shed above the trap door while everyone else was underground. This endangered all of us. My grandmother realized that with no space, no air, and no food, we couldn't survive. So, after two nights, she said that she was going to stay with a farmer she knew who might be able to hide her.

I believe that my parents knew that she was sacrificing herself so that we would have a chance to survive. She went out and never came back. After the war, we heard that someone had seen her being transported to Treblinka. That, as we all know, was a one-way trip. One story we heard was that as she was being taken to Treblinka, she tried to run away and was shot. We will never know what really happened. My mother carried the burden that her mother had sacrificed herself for us for the rest of her life. She always thought that maybe there could have been another way, but we all know that there really wasn't.

Time dragged on. Food was running out and we were becoming desperate. To add to our problems, I developed a cough. I could control my voice and not cry, but I could not control the cough. If anyone heard, we were dead. What to do? My father opened our trap door to let some air in, and lo and behold, a chicken had laid an egg right at that very spot! True, there were chickens in the area, but in all the time that we spent in our bunker, we never saw a chicken and certainly not an egg. My father took the egg, broke it into a glass, added sugar and made a "gogel mogel" (a concoction of beaten egg and sugar). I drank it and just stopped coughing. It was one of the many miracles of our survival.

We were four people hiding in a totally hostile environment. How long could we last without arousing suspicion? Not too long, it seems.

Food and water was a constant problem, especially food. Our stores had long run out, but my mother, who was on good terms with one of our Polish neighbours, managed to get a loaf of bread from time to time – just barely enough to keep body and soul together. My mother went out at night and took a circuitous route. She told the neighbour that we were hiding in the field so that no one would suspect that we were in the immediate area. After a while, the neighbour refused to buy bread for us. Apparently, she was too frightened to have anything more to do with us. We simply did not know what to do.

We had been in our filthy hole for five weeks. It had at first been hellishly hot, but it was now freezing cold – it was the beginning of November. As we absolutely had to get some food, my parents came up with the idea of sending my sister into town to buy bread. A young girl had a better chance than a grownup, so Rene went out and, to our great joy, managed to bring back a loaf of bread. We made it last a week. What to do now? Well, it worked once, why not again? So, off she went to buy bread again, but with the additional instructions to go to my father's mother's house to try and find out what had happened to her and my father's brothers and sister. She was also instructed to go to the house of our parents' good friends, the Elblings, to try and learn what had happened to them.

So, here was my sister Rene, pasty white and emaciated, hardly being able to stand on her feet after almost six weeks in our living grave, walking through town. Surely conspicuous among the blonde, rosy-cheeked, well-fed Polish girls. Sure enough, a Polish girl walked up to her and said, "I know you are Jewish; give me your money or I will tell the Germans." My sister gave her money, but not all of it. Frightened as she was, she continued on her way and managed to get to the bakery. The baker, however, said, "You are a Jew – I don't sell bread to Jews," so she left empty-handed and continued on to my grandmother's house. My grandmother had owned a store in the centre of town; it was on the town square where a weekly produce market was held. Peasants used to come here to sell their foodstuffs and buy whatever goods they needed. It was a brick building that had been in the Bielawski family for generations.

My sister came to the building that had been broken into and looted and called out my uncles' and aunt's names: "Feivel! Rachmiel! Moishe! Menucha!" No answer. She then went to the Elblings' house and went into a cellar. There was no one there. It was dark and spooky, and she thought that she saw some corpses there, although she wasn't absolutely sure.

When Rene came back "home," she saw a Polish neighbour hanging around, so she knew that she had to back away into the nearby field. She understood that no one must see her going into the shed. In the meantime, we were getting worried as it was taking her too long to come back. Finally, my father went out of the bunker and went to the back of the shed where there was a loose board (we were locked in) which could easily be removed. He called out to Rene in a low voice and when she answered, he told her to wait until it turned dark. Since Rene, of course, didn't know what to do, my mother came up with the idea of sending her to a Polish friend's house (she had gone to school with this woman and felt that she was trustworthy) and gave her directions.

The woman took my sister in and tried to feed her, but Rene wasn't able to hold the food down since she had been starving for seven weeks. The woman allowed her to stay until it became dark. As she was waiting, she saw our mother coming (it was still daylight) and became very frightened as she didn't know why she was coming so early.

Our mother explained that a very short while after Rene had left, the Polish neighbour who had been hanging around pulled up our trap door and found us all cowering in our hole. She insisted that we leave immediately. She had probably seen my mother and sister outside. My parents pleaded with her to let us stay until dark. It was impossible to leave during the daylight, as our chances of getting anywhere undetected were zero, and she finally agreed.

Luckily for us, mother's school friend agreed to let us spend one night in a root cellar in a barn which she owned. The barn was quite a distance from any habitation, so it was relatively safe. When darkness fell, my father took me on his back – I was very small and thin. He wrapped me in a sheet so I looked like a sack on his back. We left at dusk and made our way to the root cellar, which was cold and damp and full of what I believe were turnips. We ate some of them – I will never forget their smell – and spent a few cold, frightening, sleepless hours there. At four in the morning, we decided to leave and head into the forest. My father decided we should get an extra early start as he was afraid the woman might change her mind and turn us over to the Germans. So, again, I was wrapped up in the sheet, and off we went. Where could we possibly go?

My father knew a Polish man named Dudek who had been a customer at my grandmother's store. He was a big strong man with a number of equally strong sons – the kind of family no one wanted to mess with. He had told my father, grandmother, and his siblings that if there was trouble, they should come to him and that he would protect them. He lived in a tiny village called Grodzisk. But where was this village?

Into the Forest

We headed into the forest in the early and still dark hours of a cold, Polish, November morning in search of the town. After a couple of hours of going around in circles, we were stopped by a band of Polish robbers who were apparently looking for easy Jewish prey. My father recognized some of them but pretended not to know them, for recognition meant certain death. They demanded all our money and valuables, and when my father said we had nothing, they searched us. At first, they thought that the sheet in the shape of a backpack in which I was being carried was filled with goods, but when they tried to take it, I began to cry and they realized that there was a small child inside and nothing of any value to them.

They found nothing on us but they did take my father's boots. In spite of my mother's begging and pleading that my father could not walk without boots, they took them. We were lucky they didn't just kill us. My father always thought it was because they knew him; and besides, what good would it do them?

My father, who had honed his survival skills to a very keen edge, was clever enough to have sewn a number of American gold coins in denominations of five, ten, and twenty dollars into four wide cloth bracelets and placed them on my wrists and ankles. He figured, correctly, that if we were ever robbed, no one would search a small child. That decision saved our lives many times over.

So, here we were on a freezing November morning – a family of starved, dirty, hopelessly lost Jews in a Polish forest.

We found ourselves wandering aimlessly, until my father, whose feet had turned blue from the cold, could no longer walk. He just sat down, completely helpless and exhausted, thinking that this was the end. My mother, who spoke an educated Polish and could pass for a Polish woman, decided to go on by herself and see if she could find some help and come back for us. Here again, as luck (miracle?) would have it, she saw some smoke coming out of the chimney of a little house not too far away. She went up to the house and asked if anyone could help us. The farmer there said that he couldn't, but perhaps the Wojt (village elder or mayor) might do so and pointed her in his direction.

This was a tiny village called Pienki where we had stayed for a while when the Nazis first entered Wegrow. The Wojt was an older man who lived next to his spinster daughter, named Helena.

My mother made her way to the Wojt's house, spoke to him, explained our desperate plight, told him we could pay and asked if he would help us. To our great relief, he agreed. My mother and the Wojt came to get us, and soon we were sitting by a warm fire. I will never forget drinking a hot glass of milk with honey in it and eating noodles with milk. That was heaven!

My father asked him to get him some boots but to be very careful lest someone suspect that he was buying them for a Jew and thus bring disaster on all of us. Getting a pair of boots to fit my father was no mean task. My father was a small man with small feet, and boots in that area were made for large Polish peasants with large Polish peasants' feet. Within a short time, the Wojt came up with a "small" pair of boots. Still many sizes too large, but infinitely better than nothing. My father had to pad them with straw to make them fit.

The Wojt was not an altruist – he was, in fact, an anti-Semite – but the money was good. Later, that very same day, news came that the Germans were coming and we had to leave immediately. The Wojt didn't care where we went – just out! My father and sister ran in one direction, into a forest, and my mother and I in the opposite direction into some open fields. That way, at least half of us would have a chance to escape.

I remember well sitting in a green field – it was a beautiful sunny November day – beside my mother. We were watching some cows peacefully grazing, and I looked at my mother and asked her why we were always running? How was it that the cows could just be left in peace and we couldn't? Why couldn't we just be cows? My mother hugged me and cried.

We stayed there until dusk and slowly wandered back to the Wojt's house. The Germans had been and gone, but my father and Rene had not come back. It was dark and getting late and we feared the worst. Later, to our great relief and joy, my father and sister came back. They had spent the day in the woods and had had a narrow escape. They had actually seen the Germans in the distance but managed to remain undetected. Another day, another miracle. The Wojt, however, was spooked and would not let us stay. Neither bribes nor pleading helped. He was just too scared, so we had to leave. Where?

The Wojt showed us where a poor farmer who was a relative of his lived and we made our way there. His name was Tofil, but we always referred to him as Pan Tofil (Mr. Tofil), and after much begging, pleading and arguing, and after some money had changed hands, he agreed to take us. But it was understood that it was on a very temporary basis, a few days at most.

We were sure a pretty sight. After not having bathed for seven weeks, emaciated, covered with lice and fleas, I'm sure that we looked less than human to anyone who saw us. We managed to squeeze a week's "room and board" out of Pan Tofil. He was a poor man, and our diet consisted of little more than bread and water. I got an occasional glass of milk, which was just heavenly. Tofil kept us locked in a back room, while he and his wife were out in the fields, and we were hungry all day. My father, being a very resourceful man, managed to devise a way to open the door from the inside, go into the kitchen, slice a piece of bread off the loaf that the family kept in the cupboard, come back into the room and lock it again from the inside. This worked for a couple of days, but it seems that Tofil noticed that the loaf of bread appeared shorter than it had been in the morning, so he made a mark in order to be able to check if anyone had tampered with the bread.

One had to get up pretty early in the morning to outsmart my dad. Father examined the loaf, saw the mark, and after slicing off the small piece of bread, duplicated the mark further down. Tofil never caught on. After a week, however, Tofil said that we just had to go because they were too scared to chance it any longer. Again, where?

My father still held on to the hope that Dudek – the one that we had originally hoped to stay with after leaving our first hiding place – would help us. Tofil agreed to take us to Grodzisk where Dudek and his family lived. He let us off quite near the house and turned back. When we knocked at Dudek's door, we got a very cold reception. They just didn't want to have anything to do with us. Their sons were in the Polish partisans and they were not willing to take any risks for us. We could not stay – not a day – not an hour – not a minute! However, it was daylight, and we were very conspicuous in this land of large Polish peasants where to be recognized as Jews meant certain death. After much pleading, Dudek's wife agreed to sell us a piece of bread. Off we went to spend the day in a nearby dense wood until dark, when it was easier to travel.

To say that Dudek had been a huge disappointment would be an understatement. We were out of ideas and near the end of our rope. The only thing my parents could come up with was going back to Tofil. We trudged our way back, where, as you can imagine, we did not get a very warm reception, but he took us back temporarily.

At this point, news, which was related to us by Tofil, came from Wegrow that the killing of Jews was finished. Jews could and had to (by order of the German army) return to Wegrow. They would have to work, but otherwise, they would not be harmed. However, any Jew caught outside the confines of the town would be immediately shot.

To believe them or not to believe them? If they were lying, they would kill us, but what if it was the truth? What if the Germans' policy towards the Jews had changed and had become less virulent? What was the alternative? To stay on the run from the Germans who would kill us if they found us, and from many of the Poles who would only be too happy to sell us out to the Germans for a kilo of sugar or a few cigarettes? Many would have been willing to render that service to the Germans for free.

My father, who was neither naive nor trusting, decided to take his chances in the countryside. What an awesome responsibility. If he guessed wrong, we were all dead. He did, however, take advantage of the lull in the murders to sneak back into Wegrow to check on his mother, brothers and sister, and to get some money which he had buried in the vicinity.

To his great relief, he found his family alive. They too had survived in their bunker, and they had now managed to find employment at Kreda's. Kreda was a Jew who owned the only dry-cleaning establishment in town. He had been spared and believed that he was safe because he was the only one who knew how to clean German uniforms. This turned out to be, alas, only a temporary respite.

Splitting Up

When my father returned from Wegrow with the wonderful news that his family was alive, he and my mother decided that it would be safer if we split up. The plan was for my mother, sister, and me to go to Praga. This was a suburb of Warsaw on our side of the Vistula River which ran through Warsaw. My father had arranged for forged "Aryan" papers. These were documents showing that we were Polish Christians. As I said earlier, my mother could pass. I, too, being a very blonde, almost white-haired little boy and my sister, who was a brown-haired, blue-eyed little girl, would most likely not be a problem.

My father was almost a caricature of a Jew, short, long-nosed and speaking Polish with a decidedly Jewish accent. He had no hope of passing. My parents' plan was for my mother to stay with a Polish woman who would pretend to be her aunt (this was prearranged). We assumed it would be easier to get lost in a large city. In order to facilitate our trip, my father made a deal with a Polish wagoner to provide us with transportation.

On the appointed day, we said our goodbyes to father and were taken by Tofil to a restaurant nearby where wagon drivers would stop for rest and food, somewhat similar to today's truck stops. When we arrived, we sat outside on a bench and waited and waited. The day went by and he did not show up. Word finally reached us that he had gotten drunk that morning and so was in no condition to travel. We were very disappointed but could do nothing about it, so we were taken back "home" by Tofil, who was very nervous.

So, again, we split up for a while, since he agreed to keep me and my father while it was arranged for my mother and sister to stay with Helena, who was (as I mentioned before) the Wojt's spinster daughter. My mother and sister had a miserable time there. They had to spend the daylight hours in a clothes cupboard and could come out only in the dark. My father, in order to calm the Tofils down, built a hiding place for the two of us in the kitchen. He lifted up a floorboard, dug a hole in the ground, and replaced the board and put the stove over it, so if anyone came, we could quickly make ourselves invisible. However, if no one was in the vicinity, we could stay in the back room.

I remember using the hiding place quite a few times. It wasn't only from the Germans and Polish partisans that we had to hide, but also from Tofil's neighbours and extended family. We sometimes spent many hours in the hole, and my father, who had very good hands, would either fashion things out of clay (the earth in the hole in which we were hiding was clay), or carve things out of wood. I especially remember his fashioning a whistle out of clay in the shape of a bird. When you blew into its tail, it whistled. Another thing I remember is his carving an acrobat out of wood.

This toy consisted of a little wooden man, two sticks, and a piece of string. The wooden man was fastened to the two sticks (one on each side) by a string. When the string was wound and the sticks were pulled, the little man would do acrobatics. A third toy I remember was a wooden rifle that turned out especially well.

When we came out of the hole, Tofil's little son saw the rifle and wanted one too, so Tofil sat down to carve him one. It came out all crooked, and the little boy started to cry. Tofil became angry and threw the rifle into the fire. My father quickly sized up the situation and gave his boy my rifle. The last thing we wanted was to upset Tofil. I was heartbroken but understood and didn't cry. In the meantime, my mother and sister's situation had gone from bad to worse and they had to leave.

Tofil had a half-brother called Karzimiesz who lived about three kilometers from Tofil, and he agreed to take my mother, sister, and me. Karzimiesz was a religious man and a relatively wealthy farmer, so the conditions there were relatively good. How well I remember eating real food – foods that I hardly knew existed. I also used to love to watch the centrifuge for separating the cream from the milk and the churning of the butter.

In the meantime, word came from Wegrow that grandmother Sarah Frieda could no longer stay where she was and that father absolutely had to find a place for her. As I said earlier, Karzimiesz was a well-off farmer who lived in half of a two-family house. The two halves had an adjoining door, so that one could move from one to the other without going outside.

My father convinced the neighbour to take grandmother and my Uncle Moshe, and for extra protection, built a hiding place under a bedroom floor. Arrangements were made through Tofil for a farmer to bring grandmother and Uncle Moshe to Tofil and then Tofil brought them to us. That is how grandmother and Uncle Moshe came to join us.

My stay at Karzimiesz's house was wonderful, but it did not last long for me (only about a month) because he refused to keep me any longer. Perhaps he was afraid that since I was such a small child, I might cry and endanger the whole enterprise. So – to my great disappointment – back to Tofil's backroom and my father. My father and I were separated from the rest of the family for about five months.

My father used to wait until I was asleep and then make his way to Karzimiesz's farm to visit my mother, sister, grandmother, and Moshe. He could, however, not go until I went to sleep, so he used to wait until I was fast asleep and then go.

One night, I felt especially uneasy. I guess I just had the feeling that my father was going to leave me alone. I remember that my father sat beside me, waiting for me to go to sleep. I, however, fought sleep and kept stroking his arm. Being half asleep, I kept murmuring for my father not to leave me. Time passed and my father grew desperate. He finally got an idea. He put the household cat on the bed, removed my hand from his arm, and moved it to the cat. Apparently, I didn't feel the difference, and kept stroking the cat and murmuring to it.

I have no idea how much later (probably only a few minutes) I realized that I was stroking the cat and that my father had gone. I woke up screaming and crying. I woke up the Tofils in the next room who asked me what the matter was, and when I told them that my father had gone, they reassured me he would be back soon and if I stopped crying they would give me some really good food the next day. I stopped crying out loud, but kept on sobbing for hours until my father came back. He calmed me down and I finally fell asleep. I never did get the food.

This arrangement with Tofil and Karzimiesz and his neighbours lasted for about six months, at which time some of the neighbours in the area were becoming suspicious, and my mother, sister, grandmother and uncle were told to leave. Grandmother and Moshe returned to Wegrow, where they found my Uncle Feivel and Aunt Menucha at Kreda's (the Jewish drycleaner who was still operating his establishment).

My parents convinced Karzimiesz to take my sister, mother and me to the wagon stop we had been at before in order for the three of us to be taken to Praga. This was our second attempt. Again, we came and waited all day for the prearranged wagon driver, and again, for the second time (lucky for us), he failed to show up. What a stroke of luck – or was it one more miracle? – that the plan fell through. We were working on pure initiative as to what to do, for we had no idea what was going on just a few kilometers away, much less so in faraway Warsaw. Had we gone there, even if we had been lucky enough not to have been caught by the Germans, we would have had no place to go and absolutely no way to even begin finding a way to survive. We would surely have perished from hunger and lack of shelter – if not at the hands of the Nazis, then their Polish collaborators.

This time, mother convinced Karzimiesz to take the three of us back to his house and tell everyone that we had gone to Warsaw. The story sounded plausible and he agreed. We only stayed there for about three weeks, and, for a while, even our father didn't know that we hadn't gone to Praga, as we couldn't get word to him.

When word came from Feivel that Kreda's was shut down and that this spelled the end of all the Jews in Wegrow, Karzimiesz became frightened and demanded that we leave. So, we all went back to Tofil. As Tofil was uneasy keeping us in his back room, my father built a hiding place underground in the barn. Soon the rest of the family would join us.

First came my grandmother and Uncles Feivel and Moshe, and a few days later, my Aunt Menucha, who had been shot, came to join us. She told us her story. The Germans and their Polish helpers came to Kreda (the Jewish drycleaner who thought that he and his staff were indispensable to the Germans) and ordered the Jews out. My aunt was in her nightgown, and when the Germans came, she hid beneath some old boards. She told us how she had heard the crying and pleading but to no avail. Seventeen Jews, including women and children, were machine-gunned. The Germans left, but an overly zealous Polish policeman started to double check.

He found my aunt and pulled her out into the street and pointed a gun at her. She begged him to let her go but he refused. She tore out of his grasp and ran. He shot and wounded her and she fell, pretending to be dead. He looked at her, apparently convinced that she was dead, and left. After a short while, when she saw that the Pole had left, she got up and ran away. Despite her wounds, she ran until she came to the house of a man she knew. He agreed to take her in and allowed her to clean up a bit and dress her wounds. He then told her that she had to leave as he was afraid to keep her any longer. She then made her way to another farmer's house, where she was allowed to stay for another few days. Then she was brought to Tofil's, where she knew we were staying.

I still remember my father dressing the wound on her back with nothing but some relatively clean rags and water from a bottle which we warmed under our armpits. The bullet hole was an awful sight and the smell was almost unbearable for me. Luckily for her, the bullet had passed through her shoulder, so no serious infection occurred.

Figure 7: Menucha with her husband, Moshe, a while after the war.

Awhile later, Yerachmiel and his wife, Itka, came to join us at Tofil's. We were now ten people: my father, mother, Rene, and me, my grandmother, my uncles Feivel, Moshe, Yerachmiel, Itka, and my Aunt Menucha.

Tofil became frightened. The hiding place could not hold ten people. He had not bargained for so many people and he wanted no part of it. He ordered us out.

My father spoke to him and offered him a great deal of money to allow us to build another hiding place in one of his fields and supply us with food and water. After much cajoling and convincing, he agreed. The gold coins we gave him helped tip the balance in our favour. So, my father and uncles dug a pit barely big enough to hold us all and just deep enough to sit in. Tofil inspected the sight, saw that the bunker was invisible from the outside and allowed us to stay. But for how long?

There was another problem. Tofil was a poor farmer and none too bright. If he were to go to town and flash his newfound wealth around, or if he were suddenly to buy new farming equipment or livestock, he would arouse suspicion and get us all killed. Even buying extra food which he needed to feed us was dangerous. My father and uncles spoke to him and explained the danger. They instructed him not to buy all the food in one shop or stall, but to buy in small amounts in several places. Tofil, however, could not contain himself and bought some pigs or perhaps a calf. By doing so, he aroused the suspicions of his neighbours, who came nosing around and asking questions.

One evening, my father saw that there was a meeting of the Tofil clan. There were a number of brothers and half-brothers, and they were all neighbours and knew about us. My father became nervous and suspicious, so he made his way to the house in order to eavesdrop on the meeting. Sure enough, they were discussing what to do with us. The consensus was that it was too dangerous to keep us and that they should turn us over to the Germans and collect the reward. There was, however, a brother named Stefan who was, I believe, the oldest brother. Stefan carried a lot of clout within the clan. He was a religious man and said that to turn us in was wrong, and that it must not be done. No one could or would stand up to him, so it was decided to leave us alone. One never knows where one's saviour, or at least reprieve, comes from.

We knew, however, that our days with Tofil were numbered and we had to find an alternative. Besides, life in the pit was unbearable – it was much too small to hold all of us. This was the summer of '43. It was hellishly hot and we were all infested with every kind of vermin known to man. There was not enough air and the stench was unbearable.

I should say at this point that this running and hiding and conniving had become our way of life. We never lost hope and we never considered giving up. Our will to live is what kept us all going. There was no point in bemoaning our fate, as we were all in the same terrible predicament and no one else really cared. I do remember that all through the war, we tried to keep our morale up with the thought that if we could only hold out a bit longer, the war would be over and we would live. Our only concern was how to survive one more day. We took it one day at a time.

Moving On

As we had to leave Tofil's as soon as possible, my father and my Uncle Feivel went out to look for an alternative, but they could only travel at night. They searched until they came to a farmhouse that was a bit out of the way. They knocked at the door and a middle-aged man opened it. It was a man named Korczak whom they recognized as a customer of my grandmother's. He was a decent man and a devout Christian who listened to our plight, and after discussing the situation with his wife (who was not very keen on the idea), he said he would help us.

He asked how many people we were and was told six. My dad and uncle were afraid to tell him that we were ten. They figured that they would try to sneak a few of us into the hiding place without him seeing us. We all hid in Korczak's hayloft. It was wonderful. The hay smelled good and we could actually breathe fresh air. And if that was not enough, we were treated to the best food that we had had in ages – he actually killed a goose for us and supplied flour and eggs. My mother and Aunt Menucha did the cooking while Mrs. Korczak watched. The food was just too good to be true.

Still, there was a fly in the ointment. Since we were in the hayloft, we were quite exposed to the Korczak children and their friends who often played in the area, so we did not know how much longer we could stay. Our luck lasted a few days. The food was wonderful – bread, butter, eggs – real food. The man was truly a saint. We ate goose and chicken – it was incredible. We even managed to wash for the first time in ages. Soon, unfortunately, our luck ran out. A neighbour's child climbed up the ladder and peeked into the loft. If he told his parents, we were goners. Time to find another place of refuge.

Bujalski

This time, my mother and my Uncle Feivel went out to see if they could find somewhere for us to go and luckily managed to find a place on a farm a short distance away. The name of the farmer who agreed to take us was Bujalski.

We told Korczak that we wanted to pay him. At first, he refused payment, but we knew he was a poor man so we insisted. Finally, he agreed, but he refused to make a profit on us. He would only take payment for the actual cost of the food. Truly a "mensch."

When we got to Bujalski's, we climbed a ladder up into a loft in his barn where he kept his animals. It was a very long loft, running the full length of the barn. The floor was made of rough planks, and underneath, the farm animals were kept. Horses, cows, pigs, and a few chickens and geese could be seen wandering around (*Figure 8*).

He brought us some food and milk, and after the few days he agreed to keep us, we asked if we could stay longer. We offered to pay him a lot of money in gold dollars. He agreed but said that the farm was too dangerous, and so, again, the Bielawski brothers had to build a bunker out in the field. This again consisted of a small pit (really much too small for ten people), covered by planks. It was terribly crowded and hot during the day, and freezing cold and damp at night. We stayed there for three to four weeks.

Figure 8. A drawing of Bujalski's farm. The barn where we hid is in the centre.

While Bujalski and family worked in the fields, they sometimes forgot to bring us food, so we just starved until he brought us some bread.

I especially remember three incidents from this period. Once, when we were very hungry (we were always very hungry), Bujalski brought some sort of meat. When we heard that it was a rabbit that one of his dogs had killed, we just couldn't stomach it. Just looking at it put everyone off. In the end, no matter how hard we tried to eat it, we just couldn't.

The other incident that I remember vividly was the time that a little boy, perhaps twelve or thirteen years old, picked up the trap door to our bunker and saw us. We were all in a panic. If he told anyone, we were all dead. My father took a hatchet that he kept by his side and went after him, fully intending to kill him.

After a short while, my father came back breathless, and explained to us that he had caught the boy but just couldn't kill him. He said that the boy looked so terrified that my father, who had never killed so much as a chicken in his whole life, just couldn't bring himself to do it. He also said that he suspected that the boy might have been Jewish. In any case, we were very frightened for the next few days.

The third incident occurred at the end of our stay in that particular hellhole. It had begun to rain heavily, and the pit was filling up with water. If we stayed, we would surely drown; but if we went out, we would be out in the open in broad daylight.

When Bujalski came, he saw the situation and built a mound of rye around the entrance so we could go out without being seen. We then all got out. As soon as the last Bielawski got out (I think it was my Uncle Moshe), the bunker collapsed. Another few minutes and we could have been killed or seriously injured, which, in any case, meant certain death, as there were no medical facilities nor any hope of getting any medical help.

As we were standing there, looking like a bunch of ghouls – filthy, unshaven, emaciated, flea-bitten and covered with lice – we noticed that my Uncle Moshe's hair had turned green. He had been wearing a black beret, and when it got wet, the colour ran and turned his hair green. Well, we all started to laugh. All of us just laughed and laughed uncontrollably. We just couldn't stop. It was a wonderful release from the unbearable tension. Someone from the outside looking at us would probably have taken us for escapees from a 16th century insane asylum. When darkness fell, we climbed back into the loft of the barn. What could we do next? It was just too dangerous to stay there. Anyway, Bujalski would never agree to it. But we had exhausted all the other possible places of refuge.

The brothers spoke to Bujalski and convinced him that if they could build a hiding place in the barn in such a way that he couldn't find it, he would let us stay – for a very large payment in gold, of course. Well, he agreed.

The loft, as I mentioned, was very long, so the brothers built a false wall inside the loft just a few feet from the outside wall. Bujalski supplied the building materials. They built the wall in the same manner as the original wall and made sure it looked dirty and old so that it would not arouse suspicion. The entrance was a moveable floor plank which could only be reached by a ladder from the barn. When we were all up there, we would pull the ladder up, replace the plank, and be completely concealed. It seems that the only way that a Jew could survive in wartime Poland was to be invisible.

When the job was finished and most of us were in our hiding place, Bujalski was called. He searched and searched but could not find us. He then called his wife, Helena. She too searched but could find nothing. They really didn't believe that we were there. When they were shown where we were, they were satisfied with the arrangements and agreed to keep us.

This must have been October 1943. Now began months of fear, boredom and starvation. We were, of course, totally dependent on Bujalski for absolutely everything. If the news from town was bad and he started to get scared, we had to calm him down and give him some more money.

We had worked out a system whereby we always owed him money, but we always gave him some – on account, so we hoped, it wouldn't be worth his while to kick us out, as he would never see his money. On the other hand, he was always being given some money so he saw that we had the means to pay.

We were ten people (eight adults and two children) in a space the size of a small room with no furniture, not even a chair. We all sat on the rough wooden floor covered with a few lousy rags that passed for blankets. Our "windows" were two small, round holes in the outside wall. That was our light and air. The toilet was a bucket with a cover and a rag hanging in front of it. This is about all the privacy that any of us could expect. The stink was unbearable, but people will get used to anything.

We all had our own "turf." My parents, my sister and I sat in one part of the loft. My married uncle, Yerachmiel, and his wife, Itke, in another part, and grandmother, Menucha, Feivel and Moshe, in another. In the evening, the latrine bucket was lowered and emptied. Another bucket was used for drinking water – that too had to be filled. And, of course, there was the daily (sometimes much less than daily) rite of dividing out the loaf of bread.

Bread was life and thus was divided out meticulously and fairly. Sometimes we even got some sugar or salt, and that too was divided out. I never remember an argument about anyone feeling that he did not get his fair share. There was never nearly enough food, and I remember myself salivating after I had already eaten my share. My parents, of course, gave me some of theirs, but it was never enough.

I would spend many hours sitting on a "blanket" between my father's legs, with an old pillow in front of me to keep me warm. My parents taught me to read from pages of old newspapers. After I had learned the alphabet, reading came naturally to me. The only problem I had was differentiating between "b" and "d," until my father told me that "b" had a "boich" (Yiddish for stomach) and "d" had a behind. I was an apt pupil and was soon able to read even the most difficult articles. They also taught me arithmetic, which included addition, subtraction, multiplication and division.

Boredom was perhaps the least of our problems, but it was still serious. How do you keep yourself from cracking up when you are kept in a small area with nothing to do but sit and not make noise? There were, of course, endless discussions about how the war was going. Whenever Bujalski brought us rumours from town – our only idea of what was happening came from rumours – or a censored newspaper which was worth nothing, the family would sit for hours and analyze the news. We always discounted bad news as German propaganda.

Long after France had fallen, we refused to believe that "mighty" France had fallen apart like a rotten piece of cheese. We firmly believed that Churchill would save us and that 'the Russians didn't stand a chance. Only later on did we begin to believe that the Russians were actually beating the Germans. But when would the war be over? We had no way of guessing, but it had to be soon. If we could only hold out a bit longer, we would survive. The "bit longer," however, dragged on for many more months.

My father and uncles had pocket knives. As they were all very good with their hands, they spent much of their time carving objects out of old pieces of wood. Sometimes at night, they would sneak down to the barn where the horses were kept and cut a piece off a horse's tail. The hair would then be made into a brush which we could use to groom ourselves. One of these brushes has survived until today. My sister Rene keeps it in her handbag as a memento – as if she could ever forget. One of my uncles, I believe it was

Moshe, carved a fist that could be used as a match holder. My Uncle Feivel carved a replica of Bujalski's barn. That has also survived.

I was one of the family's favourite pastimes. They would tell me stories of what it was like before the War and how there was plenty to eat and real beds to sleep in and how one could have a hot cup of tea with sugar in it whenever one felt like it. By this time, all of this had become meaningless to me. My world consisted of whatever hole we were staying in at that time. At night, I used to cuddle up to my mother to keep warm. How that poor woman must have suffered to see her little boy living under such dreadful conditions! But she never failed to comfort me and did more than was humanly possible to ease my plight.

At one point, my uncles (out of pure boredom), convinced me that I was growing horns. To cure this "condition," they tied some potato peelings around my forehead with a handkerchief. Every day, they would check my forehead and "diagnose" the situation. This kept up for a number of days, until they grew tired of the game.

Two incidents concerning our total lack of any sort of medical or dental health stick in my mind. Once, my father developed an abscess below one of his molars. It grew worse and worse and his cheek swelled up. The pain was unbearable. He finally pulled out his own tooth with a pair of pliers that he must have borrowed from Bujalski.

Another time, he cut his knuckle with his knife while carving something. It became infected and he developed blood poisoning. He came down with a high fever and became delirious. We were all afraid for his life – no doctor, no medicine. The only thing that we could do was keep him as warm as possible and pray for the best. He must have had a very strong constitution, for he pulled through, to our great relief.

Once, an owl poked its head into one of our two "windows," which I mentioned earlier were small, round holes. As I had never seen anything like that before, I screamed – the only time I actually remember making any kind of noise. It was a reaction to seeing what looked to me like a flying cat. I still remember those huge eyes and curved beak. It took my parents quite a while to calm me down. I simply refused to believe that it was only a bird. To me, it seemed like some sort of supernatural phenomenon.

Time passed slowly, but pass it did. I was by now about five and a half years old, but I looked about two, maybe three. Malnutrition and terrible living conditions were taking their toll. To make matters worse, I had developed a growth on the left side of my back which was painless but was slowly growing. Here was something that no one could do anything about.

The winter of 43/44 was cold. Our rations were meager and Bujalski was getting nervous. The only break in all this deprivation that I can remember was the Christmas of

1943. We were all invited "down" to the Bujalski house for Christmas (I say invited "down" in quotes because we had to climb down from the loft in order to get to their house). It was a small, poor, Polish farmer's home, but to me, it looked palatial and the food was incredible. Real food – meat, potatoes, dumplings – truly a feast fit for a king. It was wonderful. Like all dreams, however, it came to an end. After the wonderful meal, we went back up to our hiding place. Back to our normal squalor.

We had no idea how much longer the war would last, but the family was running out of money, and there was no way Bujalski would keep us for free. What now?

The family owned property in town, so they decided to offer a piece of it in lieu of payment in gold, which had run out. Bujalski knew that the Bielawski family owned real estate, but wasn't sure how we could sign it over. He wasn't sure that it would be legal, but was finally convinced.

We were all becoming more emaciated, the growth on my back kept getting bigger, and I was getting weaker. I had become so accustomed to whispering that I could no longer talk in a normal voice. By now, I was six years old, but I looked no bigger than the average three-year-old. We kept each other's spirits up by convincing ourselves that the war would be over soon, that the Russians were pushing the Germans back, and that it was only a matter of time. But how much longer could we survive like this? We conjured up images of sitting around the table with a loaf of bread or maybe even a challah from which one could eat as much as one wanted, and all the hot tea and sugar that one could drink. We were pretty sure that we were the only (or almost the only) Jews left in Poland. Surely not many could have possibly survived.

How can one accurately recount the daily fear, the suffering from hunger, heat and cold, lice, fleas, and every other imaginable vermin, not to mention the everlasting boredom? It is a task that is beyond me.

Finally, sometime in mid-August 1944, we could hear the sounds of Russian and German artillery getting closer and closer. Bujalski and his family ran away and we were left to our fate up in our loft.

To our bad luck, the retreating Germans decided to make a stand at Bujalski's farm. They installed a field cannon right below us. They, of course, had no inkling that ten Jews were hidden right above them. We were trapped. Had we gone through all this just to die at the very end?

My father and uncles, who had always managed to come up with some sort of feasible plan, were stumped. The only thing they came up with was to jump down at night and kill the German soldiers with a hatchet and a knife.

Can you imagine what chance these emaciated, five-foot-four tall Jews, who at the best of times were not great fighters, had against Nazi soldiers – veterans of some of the toughest warfare in human history? About the same as a snowball in hell.

No sooner had the Germans entrenched themselves, then the order came to move out. Apparently, the advancing Russians were too strong for them and they decided to retreat. As they pulled the artillery piece out of our barn, we heard the officer shout the order *"aufreisen"* – blow it up! We were about to be blown to smithereens!

Again – luck, miracle, call it what you will – the Russians were coming so quickly that the German soldiers didn't have time to destroy the barn. Soon, we saw the Russians coming. We sneaked down and hid in a stack of wheat which was left to dry in the field. We could hear the Russians giving orders. We were now in Russian territory. We were saved – but were we safe?

For a summary of the hiding places that we used during our epic survival against all odds, see the accompanying table.

Table 1: Timeline of hiding locations (adapted from my sister Rene's memoirs)

	People	Place	Location	Dates	Duration
1	Family of four	under shed	Wegrow	Sep. 1942	6-7 weeks
2	"	Vojt's house	Pienki	Nov. 1942	2-3 nights
3	"	Dudek's house	Grodzisk	Nov. 1942	1 night
4	"	Tofil's barn	Pienki	Nov. 1942	1 week
5	Mother and Rene	Helena's house	Pienki	Dec. 1942	2 weeks
6	Father and Eddie	Tofil's house	Pienki	Dec. 1942	2 weeks
7	Mother and Rene	Kazimierz's house	Pienki	Dec. 1942 - June 1943	6 months
8	Father and Eddie	Tofil	Pienki	Dec. 1942 - June 1943	6 months
9	Family of ten	Tofil's barn	Pienki	June - July 1943	1 month
10	"	Tofil's field	outside Pienki	July - Aug. 1943	1 month
11	"	Korczak's loft	outside Pienki	Aug. 1943	2 weeks
12	"	Bujalski's barn	outside Pienki	Aug. 1943 – July 1944	1 year

Liberated

Some of the family thought that we should go out and place ourselves at the mercy of the Red Army. However, cooler heads prevailed. This was a front. The soldiers were, of necessity, tense, scared, nervous and suspicious. They might just shoot at anything that moved, or, if we were lucky enough to be taken in by them, we might be shot later as German spies (some irony!). So, we stayed put for a while, and then went back to the farm. We waited another couple of weeks, and when we heard from Bujalski that the Russians were firmly in control of Wegrow, we decided to go back. This was late August 1944.

We decided to leave Bujalski's in the middle of the night so that no one would see us leave. This was a safety precaution both for us and for the Bujalskis. If anyone had seen us leave, both their family and ours could have been in grave danger from the neighbours, many of whom would have had no qualms about murdering us. So, there we were, a ragged, emaciated, sick, filthy band of ten people dragging themselves to Wegrow, which was a few kilometers away. None of us could walk properly, as we were far too weak, but our willpower propelled us on. I couldn't walk at all, so my poor parents had to take turns carrying me, although they themselves could hardly drag themselves forward.

Finally, we arrived in Wegrow the next day, totally exhausted and starving. We were finally "free" – but free to do what? We all made our way to my grandmother's house in the centre of town, entered, and sat on the floor. The house had been looted and absolutely nothing remained, just the bare walls and the wooden floor.

Our first priority was food. We were all frightened of our Polish neighbours, so it was decided to approach the Red Army. We made our way to their headquarters, told them that we were Jews and that we were starving. They immediately took us to their kitchen and fed us with whatever they had. I remember eating some hot soup and bread. I must note to their everlasting credit that they shared whatever food they had with us, so not only did they save our lives by driving out the Nazis, but they also kept us alive for the first few days after we had returned to Wegrow.

We owed them even more than that, for we realized that they were our only protection from our murderous Polish neighbours. After a few extremely uncomfortable nights at my grandmother's, my parents decided that they, my sister and I, would move back to our original house which had two apartments in it. We managed to appropriate the smaller of the two, which was an L-shaped apartment with one long room and a cooking area. Again, however, the place had been stripped clean and we had no furniture, no bedding and no clothing; so, before we moved, Mother decided to go and try to get some bare necessities.

During the War, the neighbour who had discovered us in our hiding place had looted our apartment of good feather comforters, bed linen, tablecloths, warm clothes, etc. Now that we were totally destitute, my mother decided to go to her and ask her for at least some of our things back. The woman lived some distance away, so it was a very long walk (there was no organized transportation) for my mother. My father and we two children anxiously awaited her return, but as the day wore on, we became more and more anxious. The hours passed and, still, my mother did not return.

My father thought that if my mother was in trouble (as we suspected she was) and he went there by himself, he would not only be unable to help her but he would put himself in jeopardy – and then what would happen to my sister and me?

He desperately needed help, but who would help him? Our neighbours were hostile and totally untrustworthy, but my father finally hit on an idea. He went to the Red Army's headquarters, asked if there was a Jewish officer there, and was put in touch with a Jewish colonel. The officer listened to my father's problem and promptly got into a jeep with my father and two armed soldiers and drove to the house to which my mother had gone.

They arrived there just as the sun was setting and found two drunken Russian soldiers holding my mother at gunpoint. On the colonel's orders, the two soldiers who had come along with my dad beat the living hell out of them with their rifle butts and took them away. The colonel then told my mother to take whatever belonged to her, but by this time, she was so thoroughly terrorized that she said that she didn't want anything, just to go home.

My mother told us that when she got to the woman's house and explained what she had come for, the woman was not very happy. She was, in fact, very disappointed – as were many of our neighbours – that we had survived the war. She had become attached to all the things she had taken and was not at all keen to give them up. So, my mother believed, she went out and found two Russian soldiers and persuaded them to come to her house. Perhaps she offered them vodka and money. When they came to the house, they pointed their rifles at my mother and said that they recognized her as the woman who had been shooting at Russian soldiers from the church steeple in town.

My mother explained to them that she was Jewish and that we had been waiting for years for the Russians to come and rescue us. How could she possibly have been the woman who was shooting at Russians?

All her explanations, crying and pleading, fell on deaf ears. They were just waiting for nightfall when they would probably have raped her and certainly murdered her. Had my father come just a little while later, that would have been the end of my mother.

The Polish woman denied having had anything to do with the affair, although there is no doubt that she had set it all up. But we asked the colonel not to do anything about her. Even at this stage, we could not afford to antagonize the local population, for we were still at their mercy to a great extent. Through wheeling and dealing, my parents somehow managed to scratch together some beds, a table, a few chairs and other odds and ends, so that at least we had the bare necessities.

I'll never forget sitting at our own table with a loaf of bread in the middle as well as a teapot full of hot tea and sugar. This had been our dream for the past two years. We spoke about it often, and as we spoke about it, we would salivate just thinking about it. And here we were – we really could eat all the bread we wanted and drink all the sweet tea we wanted. But all we could do was stare at the food. No one was really all that hungry. The recent past was weighing too heavily on us, and our black thoughts dampened our appetites.

How does one make a living in a country still at war, where there is no economy and no stable currency? The only currency that was acceptable to anyone was gold in any form (preferably U.S. gold dollars) or American paper dollars – nothing else.

At a time like this, people go back to the time-tested system of barter. There were goods, such as blankets and shoes to be had from Russian soldiers, who were happy to sell anything (I think they would have sold their tanks and trucks if they could) for a couple of bottles of vodka – and the Polish peasants had vodka. My father would get vodka from a Polish peasant, trade it for blankets and shoes with the Russian soldiers (especially the officers), and then trade these goods for food and other necessities.

My Dad still had a few gold pieces that he had buried before the War, so he had a bit of start-up money. He was also very enterprising and energetic and thus was able to keep us alive. He also retrieved my maternal grandfather's kiddush cup (*Figure 9*), which we still use every Shabbat and holiday

Figure 9: My maternal grandfather's kiddush cup, which had been buried during the war and was retrieved.

My parents' immediate problem was what to do about me. I was small, sickly, and the cyst on my back was growing. My mother heard that there was a Polish hospital which was still operating in the nearby town of Siedlce. We travelled there and the Polish doctor drained my cyst with a huge syringe. The cyst had been full of pus. By the time we got home, the cyst had filled up again. We went back to the hospital a couple of days later. The doctor took a look at my back and said that I was too weak to have it drained again and that there was nothing he could do for me. My parents were horribly upset. They didn't save me from the Nazis just to see me die now that we were free.

The only other medical care available was a Russian military hospital a few kilometers out of town. It was, however, a military hospital that did not treat civilians. (Remember, the war was not yet over). In spite of that, my parents were so desperate that my father took me anyway. We hitchhiked on a Russian military truck. He had heard that there was a Jewish doctor there. He asked to speak to him, explained the situation and convinced him to examine me. The doctor said that there was no time to lose and that I had to have the cyst opened up, it was the only chance I had. He had me lie on my stomach, washed the infected area with alcohol – he had no way to administer anesthetic – and cut. The pain was excruciating but lasted only a few seconds, and then I remember being awash in a mixture of blood and pus. He then bandaged me up and sent me home. The only treatment was for me to drink milk and eat lots of good food. The bandages had to be changed often, as the wound was still draining. We thanked the doctor with all our hearts and headed for home.

Getting home was not so simple. We stood on the road to Wegrow and tried to stop any vehicle willing to take us. Finally, a Russian military truck stopped and picked us up. It turned out that the driver was as drunk as could be. He sang Russian songs and clapped his hands, which should have been on the wheel. My father tried to calm him down and very politely asked him to keep his hands on the wheel. He, however, did no such thing, but kept singing and clapping his hands and telling us that the Russians were the best drivers in the world, to which we readily agreed. We sure weren't going to argue with him.

Somehow, we got home. But as he approached our house, he stepped on the brake too late and bashed into a wall. Although we were shaken up, we were in one piece, so we thanked the driver profoundly and wobbled into the house.

I was put to bed immediately and remained basically bedridden for a couple of months. I was too weak to walk or play, and as I said earlier, I couldn't talk, only whisper. Worst of all, however, was that I could not hold any food down. Although food was hard to get, my father managed to get milk, eggs, and some meat. My poor mother tried to make the food as tasty as she could. She tried everything she could think of, but to no avail. The moment I swallowed something – up it came, all over the floor. I was never hungry. I tried to eat just to please my parents, but it just didn't work. My wound kept draining and I was getting weaker. It was touch and go.

Although our apartment was small, we had Russian soldiers billeted there. It was actually a safety precaution; as long as there were soldiers staying in our apartment, the chances of the Poles molesting us was greatly reduced. I remember the Russian soldiers quite fondly. They used to drink a lot, sing a lot, steal anything in sight and chase women. I guess a soldier is a soldier and basically follow the rule that if you can't eat it, drink it, steal it or sleep with it, it has no value.

Once, we had a Russian female tank driver staying with us. Her name was Natasha and she was fearless. When two drunken male soldiers came to our house in the middle of the night and tried to start up with her, she got out of bed, gave them a real talking to, banged their heads together and then sent them on their way. I have always thought of her as "Natasha the Tank."

Within a couple of months, a lady and her son who had survived the war came to stay with us. She was an acquaintance from Warsaw. Her name was Bronia and her son, Marek, was older than me but younger than my sister. At the same time, a man named Gustav Boraks, a barber by profession, also came to Wegrow. He had met Bronia's husband in the Treblinka extermination camp. They both tried to escape, and I believe that when they jumped off a moving train, Bronia's husband didn't survive.

After a short while, Bronia and Gustav decided to get married. It was hardly a love match, as the two had very little in common. Bronia was a very bright, literate woman, whereas Gustav was a totally uneducated, simple man. In those days, people were not looking for romance but for a practical way to survive, and a penniless widow with a child had little chance of making it on her own.

Figure 10. The Borakses

My father and Gustav Boraks (*Figure 10*) became partners in some of their business dealings, and I remember liking having Marek stay with us. One very small event has remained in my memory from those days. My sister, Marek and I went to see a performance of "The Three Little Pigs" in Polish. I thought that it was the most marvelous performance I had ever seen. So much so, that I can still remember one of the tunes and a few of the words. I'm quite sure that it was not much of a show, as my sister doesn't even remember going to see it, but it sure made an impression on me.

At about the same time that we were getting organized in our new "home," my uncles and grandmother opened a restaurant in what had been my grandmother's store and they managed to survive that way. Perhaps I should mention that the restaurant consisted of a few old tables and chairs. The family did all the work involved.

Getting Out

As the War came to an end, Yerachmiel and Itke went to Lodz, from there to Germany, and from there to Newbury Port, Mass. (Itke had an uncle there who helped them immigrate to the U.S.). They arrived there in 1945. They were the first of our family to leave the cursed shores of Europe. Eventually, the rest of the family made their way to Rockford, Illinois, with the exception of my grandmother who died in Lodz – more about that later. My immediate family and the Borakses stayed in Wegrow for about nine months, until the war was over and it was relatively safe to travel.

We then moved on to Praga, a suburb of Warsaw on the eastern bank of the Vistula River. Here I have an exact date, for we arrived in Praga just before the death of Franklin Delano Roosevelt on April 12, 1945. We only stayed there for perhaps ten days, but I remember having a good time with other kids my age playing among burnt-out trucks, troop carriers and tanks. Another favourite game was taking live bullets which were strewn everywhere, taking them apart, and burning the powder. We then took the caps from the casing of the bullet and hit them with a hammer. This made a terrific noise. Some of the kids even amused themselves by throwing live bullets into a bonfire –

a very dangerous game. It is a wonder no one was hurt or worse.

From there, we traveled to Czestochowa. But to get there, we first had to cross the Vistula, a very wide river. As the bridges had all been bombed out, the only way to get across was by a large boat rowed by some sturdy Poles. As I had never been in a boat before and I certainly couldn't swim, I was absolutely terrified.

On the other side was Warsaw proper – or what was left of it. As far as the eye could see, there was rubble with the skeleton of a tall building standing here and there. It truly looked like a moonscape. One road had been cleared in the centre of town, and that was the only way through the city. It was hard to imagine that this had once been the beautiful Warsaw that my parents had often described to me.

We arrived in Czestochowa and rented a couple of rooms for our short stay there. We stayed there for two weeks. Nothing very eventful happened there, except that I broke my leg and here is how that happened. My parents and the Boraks' went to Bytom for a few days to look for an apartment and left my sister in charge of Marek and me. I started chasing Marek around the dining room table, whacked my leg on one of the table legs and started to scream blue murder. Rene, who was only twelve years old at the time, didn't know what to do, so she called a neighbour who called the doctor and when my parents came home later that day, they had the doctor put my leg in a plaster cast. As soon as the dust had settled, my parents started to yell at my sister for not looking after me. Poor girl – what could she have done? It was not the only time she caught hell for "not looking after your brother properly," when it was never really her fault. I hereby apologize for all the grief I caused her. It was not intentional.

From Czestochowa, we moved to Bytom, which is in the district of Silesia. Here we stayed for about a year. ("We" means the four of us, plus the Borakses, for a total of seven people.) We managed to get a very spacious apartment on Yanta Street next to a lovely park. The apartment had formerly belonged to some high-ranking Nazis who had either fled or had been taken into custody by the Russians. In any case, the rooms were large and one of them even boasted a grand piano.

We found lots of Nazi symbols, as well as sheets of now worthless German marks which we used for play money. Since Gustav Boraks was a barber by profession, my father and he rented a store and turned it into a barber shop. My father, who had never cut anyone's hair in his life, also managed to get papers as a licensed barber. He must have bribed someone to get them.

I should explain how important the barber shop was. One had to have a visible means of livelihood in order not to run afoul of the authorities; in those days, a policeman could stop you on a whim and ask you what you did for a living. In effect, the store was a front. Boraks did indeed stay in the shop and cut hair, but one could not make a living doing that. On the other hand, my father was an excellent businessman and so he managed to do quite well. He bought and sold commodities which were hard to come by, and the store served as a place of business for him.

I was sent to Grade I. My parents registered my sister and me in a Polish Catholic school, the only kind of school that there was. I was then seven years old, and old enough and smart enough to keep the fact that I was Jewish to myself. I could speak, read and write Polish beautifully and my arithmetic was up to par (remember, I had received "home schooling" during the war). My sister, Marek (Bronia's son) and I were the only Jews in the school (*Figure 11*), and we were all registered as Catholics.

I had to go to church on Sundays (it was compulsory) and I hated every moment of it. One was supposed to cross oneself with holy water when one entered church, something that I always managed to fake. I even joined the Polish cub scouts and wore a uniform. But beneath it all, I knew I didn't belong. I was living out a charade.

Figure 11. Eddie and Rene in Bytom, 1946 (left); Marek and Mietek (right)

My friends were all anti-Semites and used to say things like, "if I saw a Jew now, I would kill him." When I asked why, the answer was that all Jews were evil and the Jews had killed Jesus. But so long as nothing concerning Jews came up, things were relatively good.

I remember one quite traumatic experience I had, when there was a Polish scout jamboree in the neighbouring city of Katowice. All the scouts and cubs were lined up and standing at attention in the hot sun. It felt like forever, until some Polish big shot (I think he was drunk) started to make a speech which went on and on. I, in the meantime, needed to pee and, as the speech went on and on, the feeling became unbearable. Here I was, in the middle of a huge field among hundreds and hundreds of scouts, and I had absolutely no place to go, until I finally did the only sensible thing that I could do under the circumstances – I peed in my pants. I still remember how terribly embarrassed I felt.

Another incident from school in Bytom I shall never forget was when another Jewish boy joined my class. I immediately recognized him as Jewish, as he was dark-haired and brown-eyed among all those blond-haired and blue-eyed boys. During recess, I came up to him and asked him if he was Jewish, and when he admitted that he was, I told him not to tell anyone if he wanted to survive.

The next morning, as every morning, began with a prayer followed by the singing of the national anthem. It was the custom for one boy to lead the class in the singing. When the teacher asked for a volunteer, the Jewish boy put up his hand and went up to the front of the room to lead the singing. The problem was, he didn't know the lyrics, and instead sang words (which he had probably learned at home) which were not complimentary (to say the least) to Poland. The teacher gave him a dressing down, but at recess, he was beaten up several times by the other boys and called a dirty Jew. This was his second and last day at our school.

It was at about this time that Bronia's sister-in-law who had survived the war with her son Mietek came to stay with us for a while with her boyfriend. Mietek was about seventeen at the time, and it was obvious that he did not get along with his mother's boyfriend. They sent him off to Israel where he was killed at Latrun, the site of one of the bloodiest battles of the War of Independence. His mother and her boyfriend, in the meantime, moved to Australia. It all happened a long time ago, but I still think of Mietek from time to time.

All in all, Bytom was not a bad place (compared to where I had been before). It was my first time in a real school, it was also the first time I went to see a real movie – I still remember it – it was Jesse James and the Great Train Robbery. Boy, was that exciting!

A funny incident comes to mind. One autumn day after a heavy rain, I saw an inviting mud puddle just waiting to be stepped into. I was on my way home from school and decided to slosh around in the muck for a while. The problem was that the puddle was quite deep and the mud very heavy and sticky. So much so, that I got stuck in it. After much effort, I managed to free one foot but could not budge the other one. So, I did the only thing that I could. I pulled my foot out of my boot and walked home with one boot totally caked with mud and a bare leg just as covered with mud.

When I got home, my mother was very angry with me for having brought in all that muck and told me to remove my boots and leave them outside the door. I removed my one boot and looked at her. She, impatient with my dawdling, decided to help me remove my "other boot." I can still see her face when she realized that there was no other boot.

All this time, I was a very skinny kid who had trouble holding down his food. If my mother tried to get one morsel more into me than I could hold down, up came the whole thing. My parents tried everything. My father even managed to get a bottle of cod liver oil, but it smelled so bad that just being near it made me nauseous. Once, my father brought an orange – the first one I had ever seen – and gave it to me. I really liked it. The trouble was that oranges were almost impossible to get and when you could get one, it cost a day's pay. I guess I had expensive taste.

Another memory: I was in church one Sunday playing with marbles on the pew instead of listening to the priest. The beadle (the one who keeps order) caught me, and what was supposed to be to my great shame, escorted me out of the church. I waited outside until the service was over and my friends came out. They all felt very sorry for me because I was sure to catch hell when I got home. I played along with them, but I, of course, was very happy to have been sitting in the sunshine instead of in the dank church. Needless to say, my parents were not overly upset.

After we had moved to Bytom, my grandmother, Uncles Feivel and Moshe, as well as Menucha and her husband, Moshe Abarbanel, whom she had married soon after the war, moved to Lodz. Yerachmiel and Itka had already left for the U.S.A. As it was impossible for us to stay in Poland, the whole family started to look for ways out. Feivel and Moshe decided to go to Belgium (possibly because we had a cousin there, but I am not sure) with the intention of bringing their mother once they got settled. Menucha and Moshe (her husband) would later go to Germany, and my father went to Vienna. We were to join him as soon as he had made the proper arrangements. All these places were only stepping stones until we could get to the New World and leave Europe behind us.

Not long after my father had left, my grandmother, who was still in Lodz with Menucha and her husband (Moshe and Feivel had already left), became ill. My mother thought she should go and help her out, so my mother and I went to Lodz by train. Rene stayed behind. On the way, the train was stopped in the middle of nowhere and some armed Poles got on the train and pulled off a number of Jews. They walked past my mother and me as we held our breath. A few minutes later, we heard shots and the train continued on its way. Our stay in Lodz was uneventful. My mother and I stayed for a few days and she did what she could to help out. The next and last time we were to go to Lodz was for my grandmother's funeral.

My father, in the meantime, managed to get a place for us in Vienna and told us to get ready to come. This was in February 1946. My grandmother had died a month earlier. My father had instructed us to bring as much food as we could to Vienna, as food was available in Poland (although it was expensive), but was much harder to obtain in Vienna.

Getting to Vienna was no simple matter. First, we had to get out of Poland to Czechoslovakia, which, in itself, was complicated. Getting passports required bribing officials with lots of money, but my father had arranged that before he left. In order to get to the Czech border, we first had to go from Bytom to Katowice and from there to the border and then on to Bratislava in Slovakia. In order to move from town to town, one needed a police permit, which we did not have. We didn't want anyone to know that we were leaving – it was dangerous. If our Polish neighbours knew that a single woman with two children was on the move, they might get the idea to rob us or even worse.

When we were ready to leave, my mother packed whatever clothes we had, took the huge wicker trunk of food and got onto the train for Katowice. My job was to carry two large tins of rendered chicken fat (schmaltz). This part of the trip, lucky for us, passed with no incident. If we were stopped, however, my mother had concocted a story that we were going to stay with a sick relative for a while. We spent one day in Katowice and I remember my mother taking us to see an opera called "Halka" (it didn't impress me) just so that we wouldn't have to wander around the streets (we left the wicker basket in a locker at the train station).

The next morning, we took a short train ride to the border. Crossing the border was a long and tedious procedure. We all had to be disinfected and we were thoroughly searched for contraband.

It is here that an incident happened that still gives me nightmares. The customs man in his impressive uniform was searching through our suitcases. When I asked him what he was looking for, he said, "gold and diamonds." Now, I knew that my mother had hidden a couple of diamonds inside a tube of toothpaste and that I had some gold coins in my shoes. Actually, they were placed in the heels of my shoes. I wasn't supposed to know any of this, but I was a curious child and always kept my eyes and ears open. I almost said, "Hey, you are looking in the wrong place; it's not there, it's in the toothpaste." The temptation to show off was very strong. Here was this big, uniformed Pole looking for something and I, a seven-year-old kid, knew where it was. I still don't know what stopped me, but had I told him, all our goods would have been confiscated, we would not have been allowed to cross the border, and my mother would probably have gone to jail.

In any case, after my mother had given the customs man a large salami, we were allowed to go on our way. I can still see myself: this skinny little kid carrying two large cans of rendered chicken fat. I also had instructions to walk and not to run so that my shoes with the gold coins inside would not fall apart. When we got to Bratislava, we were placed in a D.P. (displaced persons) camp which was run by H.I.A.S. (Hebrew Immigrant Aid Society), I believe.

The problem was that we were still within the Soviet sphere of influence and we had no documents for Vienna. We would have to enter illegally. The next day, we were put on a truck. It was bitter cold as we made our way to the Czech-Austrian border. When we got there, we had to turn back. It seems that the guards who had been bribed to let us through weren't there for some reason. Two days later, we tried again, and this time, the trucks made it through to Vienna. The only thing I remember about our stay in Bratislava was that we slept in a large barracks with lots of beds. The food was tolerable and there was a woman singing the same song over and over again.

II. Re-Emergence

When we arrived in Vienna, my father was waiting for us. After the initial hugging and kissing, I blurted out, "Grandmother's dead." He looked really shocked and pained. My mother hadn't notified him of his mother's death as there was nothing he could do and she was afraid that he might get it into his head to come back to Poland for the funeral. This would have put him through the dangerous ordeal of having to get out of Poland once again, something she didn't relish. My mother gave me a good talking-to and told me that I didn't have to dump this on my father immediately on our arrival. The news could have waited a little while longer.

My father had bought us all presents. I got a scout knife with a bone handle which I just loved (I never used it) and I still have it to this day. We were then taken to our new accommodations, which consisted of a very large room in an apartment belonging to Austrians and overlooking a green area. We shared a kitchen, washroom and toilet with the landlord's family. The furniture consisted of four beds, a table and a sideboard.

We soon learned that we were extremely lucky to have a reasonably decent place to live in, as living space was at a premium. Vienna had suffered quite a bit of war damage and the city was filling up with refugees (most of them Jewish) from Eastern Europe. These were people who had survived the Holocaust and were on their way somewhere. Almost no one stayed in Vienna permanently. Many of these poor people were crowded into the Rothschild hospital which had been turned into a temporary hostel, but my father did everything in his power to keep us out of there, for it was, to say the least, a very unpleasant place. It was filled with destitute, sick and often unbalanced people. It would be harder to imagine a more miserable group. Some had chamber pots dangling from their backpack and I couldn't imagine what they wanted those for. I suppose that when you have nothing, that is something too.

My father (*Figure 11*) told us that when he came to Vienna, he couldn't find a place to stay. Every place was jammed. He went from hotel to hotel until he found one where there was some room. The problem was that it was occupied by members of the U.S. Air Force and one could only get into the hotel if one had a pass from the U.S. military. I still don't know how he did it, but he managed to wheedle a certificate that said that my father was a "member in good standing of the U.S. Air Force." This episode has always tickled me. Imagine a five-foot-four Jewish man who couldn't speak a word of English being a member in good standing of the American air force!

Figure 12. Yitzhak Bielawski, 1954

Once he was settled, he had time to look around until he found a suitable place for us. It was not easy.

The family who owned the apartment consisted of four people: a big drunken husband who used to beat his wife (he was later arrested by the Russians for having been a Nazi); his wife, who was a Jewess who had converted to Christianity (I still have her Hebrew prayer book which she had given to my mother); and two daughters, one of about eighteen who was running around with American soldiers and therefore was rarely at home, and a younger twelve-year-old girl with whom I used to play.

Someone always had to be at home, for my parents had no doubt that if we left our room unattended for even a moment, our landlord would ransack it. This put a strain on us as we could never go out together as a family. We all took turns guarding our room, and although I was young, my parents trusted me to watch over our possessions. Sometimes the little girl tried to convince me to go out when I was alone (probably at her parents' instigation), but I would never do it.

Vienna wasn't such a bad place for me. Anything was better than Poland. I enrolled in a Jewish school (to the best of my knowledge, it was run by H.I.A.S.) so I could actually "be" Jewish and have Jewish friends. Although the school was far and we had to take the "Stadtbahn" (elevated train) to school, my sister and I were happy to do it. We took the train from Waringer-Gurtel near the Volksoper, the smaller opera house in Vienna. It was quite a pleasant walk from our apartment to the station. In the afternoon, I played in the street with the Austrian kids and soon spoke German fluently. I was young (eight-years-old) and small for my age, so I was lucky to have our landlord's young daughter protecting me. She was a pretty tough street-wise kid with whom the other kids didn't want to fight.

My mother mainly stayed at home while my father was out doing business. Business meant dealing in foreign currency and buying and selling jewelry, all of which was illegal. Then again, almost everything was illegal, and the police mainly turned a blind eye to these activities. Once in a while, however, there was a police raid and one or two of my father's cronies would have their money and goods confiscated and would perhaps spend a couple of days in jail. My father was very careful and never got caught, although there was one close shave.

The police had surrounded the area where all the buying and selling was happening (almost exclusively by Jews). My father saw what was going on and quickly made his way to the train station, but he was stopped by the police before he could get on the train. He asked the police what they wanted and they told him that they had to search him for contraband. So, he opened up his heavy winter coat and said, "Search." They searched him from top to bottom, found nothing, and allowed him to leave. My father had transferred all his money and gold into the large outside pockets of his coat, which he then opened wide. The police never bothered to search the outside pockets. Quick thinking, dumb cops, and good luck!

For those who don't know much about the history of postwar Vienna, it is important to note that the city was divided into four zones – American, British, French and Russian – and the streets were patrolled by jeeps with one soldier from each of the occupying powers. (There was actually a movie made about that era called, "Four in a Jeep"). One could move freely from zone to zone, but if one wanted to leave Vienna for the West, he had to pass through the Russian zone and this could be a problem, as each person was carefully checked and could be detained on any pretext. This only became a factor when we wanted to leave Austria.

In the summer of 1947, my sister and I were sent to a Jewish summer camp which was set up on a farm near the Austrian resort village of Sievering. As usual, my sister had the unenviable task of having to look out for me. Things were going pretty well for me, and I was having a good time running around and playing. My parents had even paid the Austrian farmer to give me extra food, which he did.

All was well until visitors' day, when our parents were coming to see us. While I was waiting for our parents to come, I walked over and watched some of the bigger boys who were throwing large pieces of wood up into a tree, trying to knock down some chestnuts. The trouble was that I got too close. A large, dead branch that was being used to knock down the chestnuts hit me in the face and broke my nose. I started running towards the doctor's office, and I ran head-on into a boy running in the opposite direction. We slammed into each other and I landed up with a huge bump on my forehead. So, there I was, with a swollen, broken, bleeding nose and a huge bump on my forehead. Just then, my parents appeared.

I said, "Hi Mom! Hi Dad!" They looked at me and did a double take. "Is that you, Eddie?" It seems that I was almost unrecognizable. Of course, my sister got hell for not watching her little brother. Poor Rene, there was really nothing she could have done.

Another incident comes to mind. My sister and I were alone in the apartment (I mentioned earlier that someone always had to be home to watch the place), and one of us (I don't really remember but I am ashamed to say that it was probably me) broke a very expensive crystal goblet. When my parents came back, they were very angry at our clumsiness and wanted to know which one of us had done it. We blamed each other and stuck to our stories. We joke about it to this day and neither of us is sure which one of us broke the goblet. We still jokingly blame one another.

Vienna was a great pit stop for us. We often went to the opera and the theatre, for there may have been a shortage of food but there was no shortage of culture. But in spite of the relatively good conditions in Vienna, my parents were anxious to put all of Europe behind us. Our first choice was the "Goldene Medina" – the Golden Land – i.e., the U.S.A. Our second choice was Canada, where mother had a half-brother (same father), twenty years her senior, with whom we had established contact.

In order to get into either of these countries, a sponsor was needed. My father worked with H.I.A.S. to try and arrange a sponsor for the U.S.A. At the same time, we asked my mother's half-brother, Benny, to start the ball rolling on our immigration to Canada. Within a few months, we received permission to immigrate to Canada, provided that we all pass the medical examination by a Canadian doctor at the Canadian Embassy in Vienna. This was a great worry as I was a sickly child and although my parents and sister thought that they were healthy, who could know what Canada's health standards were? What would happen if only I was declared unfit? Would it stop all of us?

The day came and we all left for the embassy. This was the one and only time that our apartment was left unattended, but you may be sure that my father did not leave a single valuable which our landlord could have stolen. We entered the embassy and nervously waited for the examination and the results. I think that the feeling must have been akin to a person on trial awaiting the verdict and his fate.

In we went, one by one, we were asked many questions pertaining to our health, examined and told to wait. After what seemed like an eternity, we were called into the doctor's office where he pronounced my parents and sister healthy, but said that I was not in very good shape. Nevertheless, he decided to approve our application provided that my parents agreed to get me proper medical care in Canada – a condition to which my parents readily agreed. We were going to Canada and we were ecstatic.

Wouldn't you know it, a few days later, we got a letter from H.I.A.S. stating that a sponsor had been found for us for the U.S.A. A good Jewish doctor by the name of Caplan was willing to take responsibility for us, and although my parents were tempted, they decided on Canada. We had approval for Canada, and who knew how the medical exam for the U.S. would go. Perhaps the doctor would not be so amenable. The important thing was to leave the horrors of Europe behind us.

I was often asked if Israel was not a viable option at the time. I must answer truthfully that, for my parents, the answer is "no." Israel (Palestine, as it was called then) was a small, dangerous place at war, and my parents just didn't have the energy to go into another precarious situation.

We now had to get ready to go. My father had managed to make a sum of money which he kept in U.S. dollars. He had also acquired some gold, a couple of good diamonds and some silverware. Not a fortune, but at least we would not be destitute, and would not have to be supported by our family in Canada, who themselves were not well off.

The Eastern European Jews who did the wheeling and dealing had their own language for doing business so that the authorities would not know what they were talking about. Thus, "soft ones" meant paper dollars, and "hard ones" meant gold dollars, etc. My parents sent a letter to Canada (thinking that they would understand their special jargon) and asked their family what they should bring – meaning gold, diamonds, or silver, whatever was of value in Canada. They answered that we should bring warm clothes and blankets. They did not understand our special language, and they obviously thought that they were dealing with penniless refugees (who could blame them?). My father realized that we could get no guidance from them in these matters.

My Uncle Benny was not a rich man. He was a junk peddler. He lived in a rented house with his wife and four daughters, Hilda, Shirley, Lily and Feigie. It is to their everlasting credit that they took out a bank loan to send us the boat tickets which would bring us to Canada (the tickets had to be paid for in Canada). It is especially commendable since they couldn't possibly know if or when we could pay them back. They also had to be responsible for us on our arrival.

We finally made our move at the end of 1947. We gathered all our goods and set out for the port of Bremerhaven which is in West Germany. In order to get out of Vienna, we had to get past Russian border control. The train we were travelling on was stopped on a railroad bridge in the middle of the Danube so that no one could get off, and a number of Russian soldiers came on the train and checked everyone's papers. As all our paperwork was in order, we were allowed to continue on. We all breathed a sigh of relief as we crossed into West Germany. At least we had left Eastern Europe behind us, if not Europe altogether.

At Bremerhaven, we were supposed to board a passenger ship called the "Aquitania," but when we got there, we heard that the ship had been delayed. We waited days and then weeks for the ship to arrive, but no one could give us a definite answer as to when the ship would come. In the meantime, we were living in a barracks under quite squalid conditions. We just couldn't wait to get out of there.

At the end of January 1948, we were told that there was a ship that had been converted into a troop carrier during the war and was bound for Halifax, Nova Scotia. The name of the ship was the "USS General S. D. Sturgis," and it would accept anyone who had tickets for the Aquitania and wanted to take it instead. The Sturgis was by no means a luxury liner, but it was leaving immediately. There were war jitters again in Europe, as the Russians and the Western Powers were sabre-rattling over Berlin, so my father decided to go while the going was good. (It turned out that the Aquitania, which was a much nicer passenger liner, showed up a few days later.) At last, we were on our way to the New World!

The trip across the Atlantic in the dead of winter, on a ship with no stabilizers, was no picnic. The passengers slept on hammocks on three levels in very large rooms with many people to a room. (Remember, the ship was used as a troop carrier and had not been upgraded.) Everyone was seasick and retching all the time. The smell was unbearable. The food, when one could eat, was certainly adequate, but one had to line up army-style to get it. We didn't complain, but in hindsight, there was room for complaint considering that we had tickets for a very modern passenger liner. Still, we were on our way instead of rotting on the shores of Europe.

Figure 13: The USS General S. D. Sturgis, moored pierside in Bremerhaven, Germany, circa 1949 (credit: Navsource)

It was on this ship that I had my first contact with a black man. I had seen the odd black person in an American army uniform, but I never got close to one as they looked scary to me. I didn't realize that there are people of many colours on our planet. The one I met on the Sturgis was one of the kitchen staff. He played with me and gave me a grapefruit – it was the first one that I had ever tasted. He showed me how to eat it. I don't think that I liked it very much, but whenever he saw me, he was always nice.

All in all, the journey was awful, as it was stormy a good part of the time. Once, it got so stormy and the ship listed so much that we were all frightened and extremely seasick. Only later did we learn that the captain had sent out an S.O.S. Thankfully, the ship and passengers all survived, and ten days later, we docked in Halifax, Nova Scotia, Canada.

III. Canada

It was early February, and Halifax was covered in fresh, white snow. The four of us went through immigration and customs. I was first and I carried a little case full of hard candies. When the customs official saw it, he gave me a big smile and let me through. My sister and parents were next. They carried rugs, crystal, and even a fur coat. When he saw all of this, his smile disappeared. There was nothing illegal going on here, but we were supposed to be poor refugees and we just didn't fit the bill. We all got through with no problems and were finally, officially and legally in Canada. Free at last!

We boarded a train for Toronto (a tiring journey of many hours) and our new life. One incident I remember well is that we all got hungry on the train, so we decided to buy a loaf of bread, as food was available. The only thing that vaguely resembled bread was a rectangular doughy white loaf with a consistency of cotton wool. We bought it and tried to slice it, we didn't succeed and finally had to tear it with our hands. This was our first introduction to Canadian bread – not very impressive.

In Toronto, we were met at the train station by our relatives and taken to their house on Major Street. It was, in fact, a small house in a fairly poor neighbourhood and it took some juggling to find space for the four of us, but space was found.

I must add here that my parents paid Benny back in full and brought him a gold watch as well as a diamond ring for his wife and presents for his four daughters.

I got up the next day, which was a snowy February morning, and saw black squirrels running around outside. I thought they were rats as I had never seen a black squirrel before. In Europe, I had only seen gray or red ones. After breakfast, I put on my snow suit and woollen cap and went outside. Kids, on their way to school, looked at me strangely and asked if I was a boy or girl. It took me some days to understand the question (as I didn't know a word of English yet) and to realize that although what I was wearing was acceptable apparel for a boy in Europe, it was not acceptable in Canada. Only girls dressed in the kind of outfit that I wore.

Within a couple of days, I was registered at Lansdowne Public School, which was a short walk from the house. Although I was nine years old, I was put in Grade I because I knew no English. I remember feeling humiliated to be in a classroom with six-year-olds. Although I was physically small for my age, there was nothing wrong with my mental age. I was in a strange land, surrounded by little kids who laughed at my inability to communicate, as well as at my strange clothes.

It was here that I did something that I am not proud of. I picked a fight with the biggest kid in the class and beat him (I didn't really hurt him), just to gain some status and respect. It actually worked to some degree.

When the school authorities decided that I was perhaps too old to be in Grade I, they decided to give me a test in arithmetic (there was obviously no point in testing me in English). They gave me a few columns of single numbers with a line underneath. I was supposed to add them up, but at the time, I couldn't believe that they wanted me to do something as idiotic as that. I had been taught long multiplication and division, and I was used to adding columns with multiple digits. I came to the conclusion that this was some kind of Canadian arithmetic that I didn't understand, and so I did nothing. The authorities concluded that I knew no arithmetic and, therefore, was in the right grade.

I had other problems as well. There was a black family with a number of children living next door to us. One of the boys who was perhaps a year or two older than I decided to "adopt me." This meant that he and I walked to school together and spent time at recess together. At first, I was happy to have a friend, but when I realized that he was one of the toughest kids in the school and that everyone was afraid of him, I understood that no one would pick on me, but no one would befriend me either.

Once, some kids were playing marbles and he asked me if I wanted some. I said, "sure," so he walked to the nearest kid with pockets bulging with marbles, turned him upside down and shook him 'till the marbles flew out of his pockets and scattered all over the schoolyard and then told me to pick them up. I stared at him in horror and said that I didn't want those marbles. He grabbed me by the front of my jacket and said in a menacing tone, "Pick them up!" I picked them up.

I knew I had to get away from him, but how? I therefore decided to leave for school a few minutes earlier and thus avoid him. That was a big mistake. No sooner had I got to school than my "friend" came up to me, grabbed me and waved a fist in front of my face. "If you try that again," he said, "I'll beat the living s... out of you!" I never tried it again.

In the meantime, my sister, who was fifteen years old, was put in Grade VI. In many respects, if I had it tough, she had it tougher. The schools had had very little experience with immigrant children at this point. I was the only one in my class and there was another immigrant girl in my sister's class. It was not a pleasant situation, but it didn't last long.

As I said earlier, the house on Major Street was quite crowded with the four of us living there, so my father started to look for a house for us to live in, and within two months, he found one. It was quite a nice house in a fairly good neighbourhood at 524 Manning Avenue, near Harbord Street. The house cost $8,000, but we only had to put down part of that sum. With the money my parents had left, plus a loan from my mother's brother, Benny, we managed to scrape together the down-payment, bought the house and moved into the house in the spring of 1948.

I should add that the loan was given to my father on the strength of a good four-carat diamond we had brought with us. Also, my parents rented the upstairs to Benny's daughter, Shirley, and her husband, Morrie, at a reduced rate.

My father, who had no trade, managed to get a job in a shoulder pad factory cutting cloth. Although he had never seen a cutting machine before, he was clever and had good hands, so he mastered the trade in no time. In fact, he was so good, that although he was hired at the "princely" sum of $26 a week, his first paycheck was $32. Still a paltry sum on which to raise a family and pay a mortgage, but every little bit helped.

I transferred to Clinton Street Public School and I was placed in Grade II (remember, I was almost 10 years old). My sister stayed at Landsdowne to finish the year. There are a few incidents that stick in my mind. One was when we were first learning how to spell. I had had no time to prepare, and the teacher gave a quiz. I don't remember the words – they were obviously very easy – but one of the words I will never forget. The teacher asked us to spell the word "I." Everyone laughed except me. I just didn't know what was so funny, and since I was used to spelling phonetically, I spelled it "aj" – good for Polish, not so good for English. Another time, we were given a number of difficult words to learn to spell. One of the words was "Christmas," the spelling of which made no sense to me. I just knew it had to be "Krismas." Learning how to spell was a bit difficult at first, but I soon caught on to it. Needless to say, in Math I was a whiz.

I remember being shocked that the school administered corporal punishment. The "bad" kids were given the strap (or the "slugs" in the pupils' language). This consisted of the principal coming into the classroom and standing the unfortunate pupil in front of him. The principal then stated the offense, made the boy (I never remember girls getting the strap) hold out his hand, and then hit him with a rubber strap which was about a foot long, two inches wide, and a quarter of an inch thick. It must have been very painful, as the recipients of the punishment screamed in pain every time they were hit. It sure had a sobering effect on the rest of us. The number of times one was hit depended on the offense. If a pupil moved his hand while the principal was meting out the punishment, he got an extra stroke. It was, I thought, primitive and cruel, and I still think so.

At the end of the year, I was promoted to an accelerated class where we would do Grades III, IV, and V in two years and my sister entered her first year in high school. We were both quite far behind in our schooling, but at least it was an improvement.

Making friends was difficult for the first few days after moving to Manning Avenue. I was the new kid on the block. My English was poor and I dressed funny. These problems were soon solved by my father, who understood human nature very well.

He carved a rifle out of wood and fitted it with a spring (which he got from an old roller window blind) in such a way that it shot pebbles. When the kids in the area saw that I had a "real" rifle that shot, they came around to try it, and that was the end of my short-lived lonely existence on Manning Avenue. I became an accepted member of the "gang."

There were, of course, all kinds of cultural problems to overcome. When Babe Ruth died on August 16, 1948, my friend Allan Cooper from across the street knocked on our door and told us in a tragic voice what had happened. I pretended to be terribly shocked. The truth is that I had no idea who he was. This was also a time of anti-Communist hysteria in the U.S.A. and Canada. No one could be accused of anything more despicable than being a "dirty Commie." I had a lot of trouble understanding this. For us, Communists were people with an ideology with which we didn't agree and nothing more and not the devil incarnate.

Within months, my English became almost perfect and I learned to play baseball and hockey (although not very well), I learned to eat popcorn (which tasted like straw), and to drink Coca-Cola (which tasted like cough medicine). My sister had a much tougher time making friends as she was older and had no neighbourhood gang to run around with, but she did manage to make friends with a few girls of her age.

Since both Clinton Street P.S. and Harbord collegiate were in close proximity to our house, both my sister and I came home for lunch. I remember eating lunch and listening to the soap operas on the radio, especially the ageless *"The Romances of Helen Trent"* (she was perpetually 35 years old) and *"Our Gal Sunday."*

Father was not cut out to be a salaried employee. Although he was an excellent worker, he couldn't stand being told what to do, so he started to think about going into business for himself.

At first, he thought he would open his own shoulder pad factory, since he felt that he had mastered the trade. Because his English was almost nonexistent, he spoke to one of the salesmen and asked him to go into partnership with him. At first, the salesman agreed, and my father gave his boss notice that he was giving up his job. Apparently, the boss had got wind of my father's plans and offered the salesman a raise in salary. The salesman took the raise and left my father high and dry. That was the end of the factory idea.

My father next decided to look for an empty store that he could buy and turn into a cigar store/gift shop. After searching for a while, he found one at 689 Bloor St., West. This place had had no luck. It had changed hands many times over the last few years and no one had been able to make a living there. It had been an unsuccessful business, selling used comic books just before it was put up for sale. When my father bought it, it was a derelict. Against all conventional logic, he bought the place, although my father's command of English was rudimentary. He had very little money, no business experience in Canada, and there were already two cigar stores in the same block. Father was undaunted and believed that his store would be better and nicer and, therefore, he would succeed. And so it was (*Figure 14*).

In 1951, we sold our house on Manning Avenue for $12,000 and bought the building on Bloor Street for $14,000. The building consisted of a store with a kitchen in the back and living quarters (3 bedrooms, living room and bathroom) upstairs, and although the building itself was solid brick, it was a mess inside. Father and Mother worked day and night to make the apartment livable and to make the store appealing. They did all the work themselves as we couldn't afford workers. My father even laid a new floor of red and white tiles, and then he bought the furnishings. He stocked the store (on credit) with gifts, chinaware, toys, cigarettes, magazines, ice cream, pop, chocolate, and many, many other items.

Figure 14. My parents in front of their store

One small incident which impressed my Dad was how easy it was to get a license to open the store. My Dad went down to the city hall, paid $12.00, and got a license to operate the store. This was absolutely unbelievable to him. In Poland, he would have had to pay a huge amount of money, bribe countless officials, and then he might have had to wait for months if not years for a license. Canada was wonderful!

As it turned out, the store did well against all odds. Although the work was hard (16 hours a day, 7 days a week), my father loved it. It was his baby, he thought of it, built it, nurtured it and it thrived. He was his own boss. Within a couple of years, he bought another building (a store and two apartments) which he rented out. Money, for father, was to be invested and not to be left in the bank.

Business was quite good until Honest Ed's (a discount store) opened about six years later, just three blocks down the street. At first, it was small and of no consequence, but it soon grew into a monster which cut deeply into our sales. We simply could not compete as there were many items which he could sell cheaper than we could buy.

My father started to think about moving on. It was not to be. On Christmas Eve, Dec. 24, 1959, on the busiest day of the year, he suffered a massive heart attack and was rushed to the hospital, where he died in the early hours of the morning of Dec. 25.

We were all in shock, as my father had never been sick and was extremely active. The man who had pulled us through the war was dead at the age of 53. It is almost unbelievable what he managed to accomplish in his short life. He was a very bright man of vision, courage and had a great belief in himself. He was always optimistic and never let circumstances, no matter how desperate, defeat him.

His brothers and sister, who were all in shock, came to Toronto for the funeral which was a very sad affair indeed.

At the time, I was attending Waterloo University. I was in the first year of a General Science course. After my father died, I basically dropped out of school. I was feeling very low and I felt incredibly lost and I felt I had to be at home to help my mother. To be fair, my mother did not at all pressure me to do this.

Business was bad and we barely eked out a living from the store. We just did not know which way to turn. On top of all this, my sister was awaiting the birth of her first child. Rene had been on a trip to Europe and Israel and had met and married an Israeli named Aaron Cohen. She came back to Canada pregnant and awaited permission from the immigration authorities to bring her husband to Canada. He finally received the proper papers and immigrated a few months later.

Rene gave birth to a beautiful baby girl on January 28, 1960, whom she named Grace after our maternal grandmother, Gittel. What a shame that my father never got to see her or any of his subsequent grandchildren.

When Aaron, Rene's husband, came a few months later, they moved out and rented an apartment. My mother and I were left alone to run the store. I took the next year off as well, but in 1960, I returned to school and got my B.A. in English. My mother, in the meantime, worked out a system for running the store by herself. I came home on weekends to help.

In the summer of 1961, a friend of mine and I drove to Mexico and the Western United States. Although it was an exciting trip, this is not the time to write about it. Things kept going pretty much the same way. My mother worked in the store and I was away at school. In 1963, I completed my studies, then took a year off and together with the same friend I had gone with to Mexico, set out for Europe where we hitchhiked through Western Europe, Morocco and Israel. This was the experience of a lifetime, but again, I do not want to elaborate here. As much as I enjoyed the trip, my conscience was not clear as I felt that I had left my mother alone in the store, although it was with her blessing. So, it was with a feeling of great relief that I received a letter from my mother telling me that she had sold the store.

Epilogue

I returned to Canada in 1964 in time to enter the Ontario College of Education, where I received teaching certificates in English and Theatre Arts.

The following year, I met a lovely young lady named Elaine Silver at a social gathering. Our courtship was short and we married on Dec. 29, 1965.

Our daughter, Frances (who now calls herself Sharon, which is her middle name), was born on February 9, 1967. Elaine and I had planned on moving to Israel in July 1966, but when we learned that we were expecting, we postponed our aliyah to July '68.

Our absorption in Israel went smoothly, all in all, and we adjusted well to our new surroundings. I became a high school English teacher and taught in Netanya for over 35 years. My wife, Elaine, who is a dental hygienist, practiced in Netanya and Kfar Shmaryahu for almost 30 years. Our son Yitzhak (Tzachi) was born on July 10, 1967, and our son Shlomo (Shlomi) on January 2, 1973.

At the time of writing, our three children are married, and they and their families are all living in Israel. Frances, who married Jonathan Bakst (a lawyer), is a high school English teacher. Tzachi, who married Efrat Chen, is working for a large computer company. And Shlomi, married to Adi Koren, is a lawyer for the Ministry of Justice. We have ten wonderful grandchildren. Frances and

Jonathan have three: boy/girl twins, Noa and Nadav, and another girl, Hadas. Tzachi and Efrat have two girls, Elia and Tamar, and a son, Raphael Yotam. Shlomi and Adi have four children: Noam, Yaeli, Itamar and Yehonatan.

Nothing can make up for the horrors of the war years. If there is any consolation, it is to be found in the fact that Hitler's 1,000-year Reich was trashed within a few years and Hitler committed suicide in a bunker in Berlin. The Jewish people lives on, and Israel, the ancient homeland of the Jewish people, is a vibrant democracy. We who survived the Holocaust must never give Hitler the posthumous victory of giving up. We must go on, have children, and raise them as proud Jews who must never forget their heritage and history.

Made in the USA
San Bernardino, CA
11 March 2018